100 Great Hikes
in and near
Palm Springs

Text and Photography by
Philip Ferranti

with

Hank Koenig
cartographer

WESTCLIFFE PUBLISHERS

www.westcliffepublishers.com

ISBN 1-56579-349-8
Text, Maps, and Photography Copyright: Philip Ferranti, 2000. All rights reserved.

Copy Editor: Nancy Hall
Designer: Rebecca Finkel, F + P Graphic Design, Inc.; Boulder, CO
Production Manager/Illustrations: Craig Keyzer

Published By:
Westcliffe Publishers, Inc.
P.O. Box 1261
Englewood, CO 80150
www.westcliffepublishers.com

Printed by: Vaughan Printing

Library of Congress Cataloging-in-Publication Data
Ferranti, Philip, 1945-
    100 great hikes in and near Palm Springs / by Philip Ferranti ; with Hank
Koenig, cartographer.— [Rev. ed.]
      p. cm.
    Rev. ed. of: 75 great hikes in and near Palm Springs and the
Coachella Valley. c1995.
    Includes index.
    ISBN 1-56579-349-8
    1. Hiking—California—Palm Springs Area—Guidebooks. 2. Hiking—
California—Coachella Valley—Guidebooks. 3. Palm Springs Area (Calif.)—
Guidebooks. 4. Coachella Valley (Calif.)—Guidebooks. I. Title: One hundred
great hikes in and near Palm Springs. II. Ferranti, Philip, 1945- 75 great hikes
in and near Palm Springs and the Coachella Valley. III. Title.

GV199.42.C22 P345 2000
917.94'97—dc21   00-020677

For more information about other fine books and calendars from Westcliffe Publishers, please call your local bookstore, contact us at 1-800-523-3692, write for our free color catalog, or visit us on the Web at **www.westcliffepublishers.com**.

Cover Photo: Agave in bloom below Santa Rosa Mountain.
Photo © George Wuerthner.
Back Cover Photo: Lush palm trees like these in Anza-Borrego Desert State Park dot the landscape in the Palm Springs area. Photo © George Wuerthner.

Please Note: Risk is always a factor in backcountry and mountain travel. Many of the activities described in this book can be dangerous, especially when weather is adverse or unpredictable, and when unforeseen events or conditions create a hazardous situation. The author has done his best to provide the reader with accurate information about backcountry travel, as well as to point out some of its potential hazards. It is the responsibility of the users of this guide to learn the necessary skills for safe backcountry travel, and to exercise caution in potentially hazardous areas. The author and publisher disclaim any liability for injury or other damage caused by backcountry traveling or performing any other activity described in this book.

Acknowledgments

Special thanks to Les and Shirley Larson
for first introducing me to the local trails.

Many thanks to Sheila Koenig for her artistic
map layouts.

Much appreciation to all the hike leaders
and support volunteers in the Coachella
Valley Hiking Club for sharing the joy of
hiking these magnificent trails.

Bruce and Denice Hagerman deserve special
recognition for their contributions to the first
version of this book, *75 Great Hikes in and
near Palm Springs and the Coachella Valley,*
published by Kendall/Hunt Publishing
Company, Dubuque, Iowa.

Table of Contents

San Jacinto Mountains

Orocopia Mountain Wilderness and the Chuckwalla Mountains

Appendices

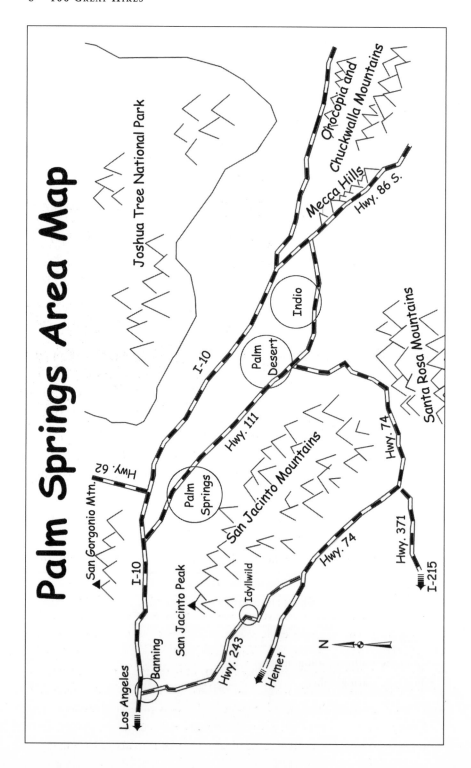

Palm Springs Area Map

Introduction

The Topography

This hiking guide takes you into the interior of Southern California, where the mountains slope down into deserts and reach out into canyons and the surrounding low foothills to form the 60-mile stretch of land known as the Coachella Valley. The San Andreas Fault cuts through this valley, contributing to its formation while causing those infamous earthquakes.

Tahquitz Peak and South Ridge Trail

The northwest area of the Coachella Valley is bordered by the San Bernardino Mountains, with Southern California's tallest peak, San Gorgonio (11,501 feet), acting as the sentinel guarding the San Gorgonio Pass which ushers visitors into the valley from the west.

The southwestern-to-west boundary of the valley is marked by the towering San Jacinto Mountain Range and San Jacinto Mountain, whose 10,800-foot massif fills the whole western skyline above Palm Springs. These same mountains provide the granite bedrock upon which the Desert Divide Ridge has been married to the Pacific Crest Trail (PCT), allowing hikers to traverse the entire 60-mile length of the mountains above the valley, all the way to Idyllwild, past San Jacinto Mountain and eventually across the pass to the awaiting San Bernardino Mountains.

Looking south by southeast, one sees the Santa Rosa Mountains, with the twin peaks of Santa Rosa and Toro dominating the horizon above La Quinta and Palm Desert. Lesser foothills carve their way along the valley floor to enfold the cities of Rancho Mirage and Cathedral City and the eastern side of Palm Springs.

To the north, the Little San Bernardino Mountains, Indio and Mecca Hills, and the Cottonwood and Orocopia mountains complete the border of the Coachella Valley and provide an abundance of canyons and interesting geological formations for hikers to explore.

Both the Santa Rosa and San Jacinto mountains are relatively new, perhaps 20 million years old. They were formed when the Pacific Plate began to push against and into the North American Plate, causing forces deep within the crust to uplift these ranges, while dredging up 500-million-year-old rocks to cover their slopes as granite boulders and sharp escarpments.

Across the valley, along the Mecca Hills, the San Andreas Fault has contributed to the valley formation by pulling the floor away

The Red Canyon, nearly 12 miles in length, is at the heart of the Orocopia Mountain Wilderness

from the southern mountains, thereby widening the valley, which acts as a receptacle for the sand deposits from the surrounding mountains' eroding granite and quartz rocks.

Thus, within 70 miles of Palm Springs, more then a dozen mountain ranges and foothills provide the raw material for 750 miles of hiking trails, making this area one of the premier winter hiking destinations in the United States.

Climate and Weather

The Coachella Valley represents the furthest reaches of the Colorado Desert. The mountains surrounding the valley to the west effectively block Pacific storms from unleashing their full potential. Annual rainfall amounts may reach 3 to 5 inches, whereas Los Angeles receives 15 to 25 inches. Hikers need to respect the desert conditions in planning where they will hike, at what altitude, and when. What begins as a comfortable 70 degree sunrise hike, might end up at 100-plus degrees by late afternoon.

Usually hikers can begin comfortable day hikes on the valley floor and in the lower foothills by November. The moderate temperatures allow hikes up to 6,000 feet in elevation all winter long, with only scattered, thin snow conditions at worst. By April, hikes should be planned for the higher elevations only. Short hikes from sunrise until morning heat sets in can safely be done along the desert floor and in the mountain canyons through late spring.

San Gorgonio Mountain as seen from the Coachella Valley

From June to mid-October, hikers can comfortably do all the 6,000- to 10,000-foot-elevation hikes. Sometimes during the dead of summer, when the Coachella Valley experiences 110 degree days, hikers can enjoy the many hikes along the PCT, and the Desert Divide Ridge overlooking the valley, in 70 degree weather provided there is a cool, onshore Pacific breeze blowing and the marine layer has penetrated inland from the coast.

In the Idyllwild–San Jacinto Mountain region, summer storms can suddenly gather and deliver a cold rain or even hail upon unprepared hikers. It is always wise to check the local forecast for the weather that might be affecting the day's hike. Still, the combination of mountains and adjacent deserts allows year-round hiking within 70 miles of the Coachella Valley—following the simple rule of thumb, "as temperatures rise, climb to higher elevations to hike."

Flora and Fauna

The Coachella Valley and nearby mountains reward the hiker with a generous diversity of plant and animal life. Dozens of cactus species, yucca, ocotillo, sage, smoketree, and desert flowers sweep up from the valley floor to the surrounding foothills and join with ribbonwood, manzanita, juniper, and scrub oak. They, in turn, eventually encounter pine, fir, cedar, and oak, which blanket the mountains and provide an incredibly distinct and fragrant "desert-mountain" scent that is unique to this area.

Lower Palm Canyon

Bighorn sheep, coyotes, golden eagles, red-tailed hawks, rabbits, deer, and even mountain lions are just a few of the animals found along our trails. Visits to the Living Desert and the Palm Springs Desert Museum yield a rich educational experience for anyone wanting to learn about the local plant and animal life.

Please note: As of this printing, the Bureau of Land Management (BLM) and other agencies have encouraged partial trail closures from January to June to protect the bighorn sheep during their annual lambing season. The trails most likely to be affected are North Lykken in Palm Springs, Cathedral Canyon Trail in Cathedral City, Art Smith and Carrizo Canyon trails in Palm Desert, Boo Hoff Trail, and the Bear Creek Canyon and Guadalupe trails in La Quinta. For more specific information, please call the BLM at (760) 251-4800.

Using this Book

At the top of each hike is found useful information for planning your hike. This mini-guide includes:

Length: Either given in round-trip mileage or one-way. If a shuttle is necessary, this is indicated in the text.

Season: The best time of year to hike a given trail in relative comfort. Please understand, however, that desert hiking is an iffy proposition—we have seen 95 degree temperatures in February and

The uplifted hills of Box Canyon

70 degrees in April! A good precaution during the warmer months is to start early, thereby avoiding the possible surge in temperatures by mid-afternoon.

Hiking Time: An estimate based on a 2 to 2.5 mph pace with some time considered for breaks and lunch. We have found that going uphill takes at least 25 percent longer than going downhill. This calculation is included in estimated times. Note that most hikes in this guide end by going downhill.

Information: Provides the name and current phone number of the agency where you can obtain maps, guidebooks, and advice for your hike. (The California Desert Protection Act of 1994 affects your access and use of Bureau of Land Management land. Consult with the BLM agency in Palm Springs for additional information.)

Elevation Gain/Loss: Measured from the beginning of the hike to the end, including the return. Hikers need to know their own stamina, endurance, aerobic conditioning levels and the like, before attempting any hike—especially the strenuous ones.

Difficulty: A relative term, but considers all of the above factors.

The tranquil pools at Lost Paradise ensure this as a favored lunch spot

This book uses the Coachella Valley Hiking Club standards as follows:

Easy: up to 500 feet elevation gain and up to 6 miles in length.

Moderate: between 500 and 1,800 feet elevation gain and between 6 and 10 miles in length.

Strenuous: over 1,800 feet elevation gain, and between 8 and 15 miles in length, or longer.

All hikes in this book are "day hikes," but many can be taken over several days if the hiker wishes to camp out.

Some trails are deceptive in their demands. A hike 6 miles in length is usually considered easy, but when most of the elevation gain comes during the return portion's last 2 miles, it might be regarded as a moderate hike. On some hikes the strenuous portion comes all at the very beginning, while the remaining 80 percent is moderate or even easy, for example, the Zen Center Trail. Some hikers find steep downhill sections more difficult than uphill, because of knee or toe stress.

Using Your GPS Receiver with this Book

The maps in this book were created by hiking the trails with a handheld Global Positioning System (GPS) receiver.

On many of the hikes the trails are obvious, and you need do no more than use your eyes. Some hikes, however, take you off trail where markers are not clear. This is when a GPS receiver can be useful. Any inexpensive ($100-$150) receiver (Garmin, Eagle, Magellan, etc.) will work just fine.

All points of interest have latitude (LAT) and longitude (LON) coordinates shown. These coordinates can be entered as waypoints into your GPS receiver. You can then navigate to each point. You can also use the coordinates to locate the points of interest on a topographic (topo) map.

Important: A datum is a reference surface on which a map is drawn. Be sure to set your GPS receiver to the *North American Datum of 1927*. This matches the datum of the local topo maps and is the datum used in developing the maps in this book, which include LAT and LON coordinates in areas that are particularly difficult to navigate. If you use any other datum, your GPS receiver will display wrong positions—wrong by several hundred feet!

Set the units of LAT and LON on your GPS receiver to degrees, minutes, and decimal minutes. This method is much easier to use than degrees, minutes, and seconds. Incidentally, the third decimal place of minutes (0.001') equals about 8 feet of horizontal distance. The second decimal place (0.010') equals about 80 feet.

Unavoidable errors: You may find that when you stand at a point of interest, your GPS receiver displays coordinates that differ from the coordinates in this book. The difference could be as much as 300 feet horizontal (0.040') but is usually less.

This difference is unavoidable and does not mean that your GPS receiver has been zapped by aliens or that the mapmaker was under the influence of illegal substances. The difference is due to a security system devised by the U.S. Government. The data collected while making the maps were subjected to differential correction, which gets around the security system. If the idea of differential correction really interests you, see Appendix 4 for a detailed discussion.

If you just want to hike and enjoy the security of knowing where you are, get out the boots, call your favorite hiking partner, fire up the GPS and start walking.

Safety

Desert hiking requires more safety than a casual walk along a national park trail. Water is essential to survival, and no hiker knows what events await on

On the trail above Painted Canyon

the trail. I suggest carrying at least 2 quarts of cool water for hikes up to 6 miles, and more water for longer distances. During the hot season you might try freezing 50 percent of your drink—for example, Gatorade or a sport drink—then adding the remainder of cool liquid the morning of the hike. This ensures a cool drink all day!

Protect your head with a hat of some sort, use sunscreen, and carry extra food and water, sunglasses, a windbreaker for the higher elevations, and basic first aid essentials like aspirin, tweezers, Band-Aids, moleskin, and anything else you feel supports your personal safety. Carry a comb in case you brush against a cholla cactus (guide the comb down through the thorns and flick off the entire ball of cactus).

The beauty of these areas demands respect. If you pack it in . . . pack it out!

It's always a good idea to have a map of the area where you are hiking, as well as a compass to assist in land navigation. The Coachella Valley Trails Council with the BLM has published a good trail map of the area.

It's always a good idea to hike **with someone else!** In case of injury or if you get lost, two or more hikers are better than one. Let someone know where you are going and when you expect to return. The Coachella Valley Hiking Club, (760) 345-6234, conducts guided hikes all year long and has hiked every trail mentioned in this book. Give them a call for information and consider accompanying them on a hike as a guest.

Wild animals present little hazard. Snakebites are best avoided by looking carefully around wherever you intend to sit, rest, or eat, and be sure not to put your hand under logs, rocks, and bushes. Wearing long pants is another protection against snakebites; despite hitting you in a strike, the snake may be unable to get enough clean leverage and angle to pierce your pant material. Mountain lions have been observed in the desert and mountains nearby, but again, traveling in numbers almost ensures that no harm will befall you.

During summer months hiking at higher elevations can be quite pleasant, with temperatures reaching into the low 80s. In August and early September,

Cholla cactus

however, summer storms can blow up quickly over the mountains. Rain gear and a warm, long-sleeved, light jacket will prove ample protection.

The Coachella Valley Hiking Club (CVHC)

In October 1992, the Coachella Valley Hiking Club was formed for the purpose of organizing hikes into the magnificent deserts and mountains surrounding the Coachella Valley, and educating the public about the availability and nature of the great hiking trails found there. The club welcomes visitors as guests for day hikes, and you can readily get information by calling their number, (760) 345-6234. CVHC is very active and sponsors over 300 hikes a year.

A Hiking Philosophy

Hiking is what our ancestors did effortlessly as part of their daily routine. Hunting and migrating to new pastures, warmer climates, and homelands are part of the psyche of human beings. We feel "home" where nature draws us into her beautiful deserts, mountains, canyons, prairies; along seashores,

Ocotillo in bloom

lakes and rivers; under star-canopied skies . . . wherever the plant and animal kingdoms engage the nurturing earth.

The advent of civilization greatly impacted our commune with nature. Cities enclosed us. Still, the call of the wild is meant for all people, eliciting primeval stirrings and beckoning us to the peace of the land's quiet beauty. Hiking is our entrée into the nurturing embrace of nature. We shed the stresses, the onslaughts of media encroachments, and the demands and noise of "civilization" when we hike out into nature and release their demanding grip on our longing hearts and spirits.

Hiking is best approached as a way of life, a creative lifestyle, part of the daily fabric of existence. To walk each day somewhere touched by nature's gentle hand, to hike each week into the calming embrace of nature . . . these are goals worthy of those pursuing a high quality of life. Trails are like a collection of recipes that only nourish when acted on; they are meant to be walked, not merely acknowledged.

The rewards are great. A moderate hike burns almost 400 calories per hour. Six hours on the trail goes a long way towards firming, toning, and weight reduction. Hiking rejuvenates and energizes the hiker mentally, emotionally, physically, and spiritually. It offers us the needed beauty of nature, teaches us her quiet lessons, and reminds us that there awaits a shelter from any of life's storms.

Santa Rosa Plateau Preserve offers a landscape of chaparral, oak woodlands, and the state's finest bunchgrass prairie

Hiking is a metaphor for life itself: We climb our inner mountains and seek quiet meadows within our souls, following whatever guide proves worthy of our allegiance. Unlike so many modern activities, a day on the trail has a set beginning, middle, and end. By trail's end we accomplish something of real value while participating in an activity free from pretense, contrivance, and bravado. Hiking is honest.

Along the trail we can share something of ourselves with our fellow travelers. The community of humankind is built on small but precious acts of sharing such as those that take place while on a hike.

This book is therefore an open invitation to visit those unique and beautiful desert, canyon, and mountain trails in and near the Coachella Valley. Ask any hiker who has been there, "What is out there?" Come see for yourself. Come reach beyond your daily routine and enjoy!

> # "If you pick 'em up, O Lord, I'll put 'em down."
>
> Anonymous
> *The Prayer of the Tired Walker*

Mecca Hills/Box Canyon
Hikes 1 – 7

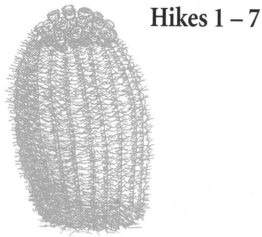

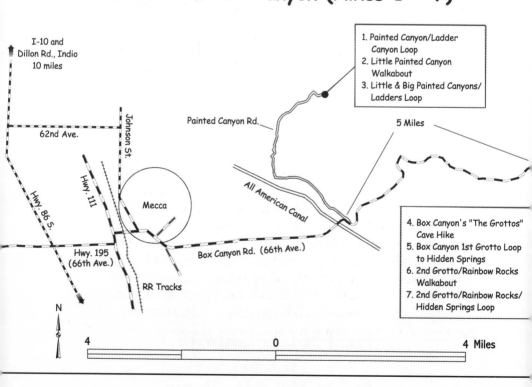

Trailhead Locations in the
Mecca Hills/Box Canyon (Hikes 1 - 7)

I-10 and
Dillon Rd., Indio
10 miles

62nd Ave.

Johnson St.

Painted Canyon Rd.

5 Miles

1. Painted Canyon/Ladder
   Canyon Loop
2. Little Painted Canyon
   Walkabout
3. Little & Big Painted Canyons/
   Ladders Loop

Hwy. 111

Hwy. 86 S.

Mecca

All American Canal

Hwy. 195
(66th Ave.)

Box Canyon Rd. (66th Ave.)

RR Tracks

4. Box Canyon's "The Grottos"
   Cave Hike
5. Box Canyon 1st Grotto Loop
   to Hidden Springs
6. 2nd Grotto/Rainbow Rocks
   Walkabout
7. 2nd Grotto/Rainbow Rocks/
   Hidden Springs Loop

N

4   0   4 Miles

1

Painted Canyon/ Ladder Canyon Loop

LENGTH: 5 miles

HIKING TIME: 3 – 4 hours

ELEVATION GAIN: 450 feet

DIFFICULTY: Easy/moderate

SEASON: October to April

INFORMATION: BLM Office, Palm Springs, (760) 251-4800

Colorful hills line the San Andreas Fault

The Mecca Hills lie in the northeast corner of the Coachella Valley, along the boundary of the North American Plate. Here the San Andreas Fault converges with several other earthquake fault lines to form the uplifted low hills known as the Mecca Hills. These hills, along with the surrounding mountains, strike the eye of any visitor as a place "off-planet," resembling a lunar landscape, especially under the soft light of a full moon. By day, however, this contorted, compressed land is blessed with a profusion of vibrant color, the result of minerals deep in the earth having been exposed over aeons of time to the erosion of wind and water, while abundant iron-based minerals have combined with the elements to form washes of red, lilac, orange, coral, and other desert hues more reminiscent of southern Utah than California. Cutting through the middle of this colorful, twisted, exotic landscape is Painted Canyon, accessible in all its mystical beauty by a loop hike using a series of ladders to reach the uplifted Painted Canyon area.

DIRECTIONS

To reach the Mecca Hills, Painted Canyon, and Box Canyon area, take I-10 several miles past Indio heading east. Take the 86 S Expressway exit towards Brawley; this new, down-valley expressway bypasses the old Hwy. 111. After turning right onto the 86 S Expressway, travel nearly 10 miles to 62nd Avenue. Turn left onto 62nd Ave. and drive several miles until reaching Johnson St. Turn right and drive several miles to 66th Avenue. There turn left onto 66th Ave. (Box Canyon Rd.). Proceed almost 5 miles past many grape and citrus ranches, cross over the All American Canal, and look for the green sign on your right indicating Painted Canyon. Turn left onto this dirt road and proceed almost 4 miles. The sign indicates passibility only for 4WD vehicles, but in dry years the road can be driven safely with a car. Check with the BLM Office in Palm Springs for road conditions at (760) 251-4800. The last mile of Painted Canyon Road passes through the beautiful and exotic canyon entrance to this area and actually crosses over the San Andreas Fault as you enter the canyon, ending at a turn-around parking area with a sign posted "End of Maintained Road". Begin the Painted Canyon/Ladder Canyon Loop Trail by walking into the large canyon marked by steep, dark, lilac-colored walls located right of the road sign and behind the BLM sign. *A word of caution:* The ladders in Ladder Canyon are sometimes maintained by volunteers. Be very careful climbing them, and if you judge something unsafe or doubt your ability, try doing the Little Painted Canyon Loop instead. It is safest to have your group's best "ladder climber" proceed up the tallest ladders first, then lend a helping hand to climbers below. Also, be careful not to get too close to the rim to look down into the canyon. Sand can be loose and slippery.

After walking 0.25 mile up the canyon, you will notice a signpost to the right that points across the canyon to the left. Walk across the canyon as the signpost directs and climb up the right side of what looks like an impassable rock slide. This trail follows the collapsed canyon along its right side until you quickly reach the first and tallest ladder. At the top the trail then takes you through a magnificent slot canyon, so named because of its thinness, and continues rising toward the top of the canyon after you've negotiated several smaller ladders. After another 0.25 mile the canyon splits, but stay right for another 50-plus yards while looking to the right for a spot that is somewhat flat and low enough to climb onto. A makeshift trail sometimes marked by a cairn brings you steeply up the side of the mud hills above the canyon; you'll have to negotiate a ledge

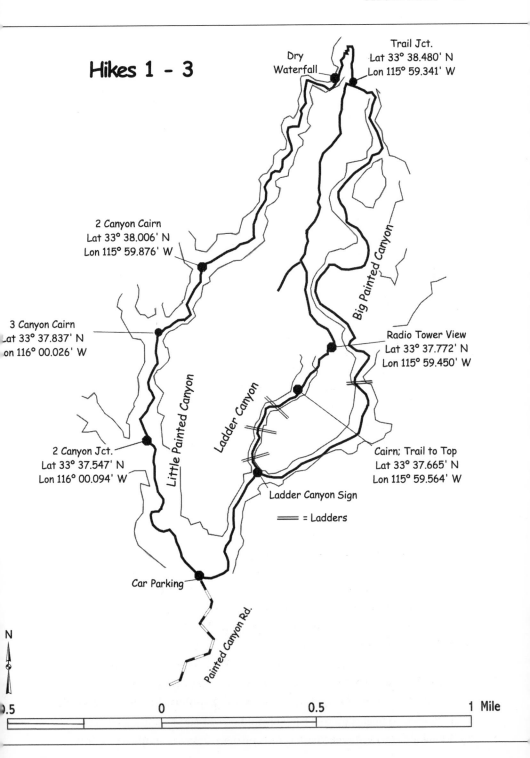

Hikes 1 - 3

Dry Waterfall

Trail Jct.
Lat 33° 38.480' N
Lon 115° 59.341' W

2 Canyon Cairn
Lat 33° 38.006' N
Lon 115° 59.876' W

Big Painted Canyon

3 Canyon Cairn
Lat 33° 37.837' N
Lon 116° 00.026' W

Radio Tower View
Lat 33° 37.772' N
Lon 115° 59.450' W

Little Painted Canyon

Ladder Canyon

2 Canyon Jct.
Lat 33° 37.547' N
Lon 116° 00.094' W

Cairn; Trail to Top
Lat 33° 37.665' N
Lon 115° 59.564' W

Ladder Canyon Sign

═══ = Ladders

Car Parking

Painted Canyon Rd.

N

0.5   0   0.5   1 Mile

several feet high before continuing up the steep slope to the top. Once at the top, take the trail to the left heading up. The trail now begins to skirt the top edge of Painted Canyon. In just a few yards you top out above Painted Canyon to the east and below you. From there you get your first glimpse of some radio towers to the north, which the trail now takes you toward (GPS). Views of the Salton Sea and the surrounding Santa Rosa and San Jacinto mountains get ever more spectacular as the trail climbs to the highest elevations. After a mile you will see ahead of you the grouping of radio towers. Note that the trail now takes a sharp right turn down into Painted Canyon.

Once in Painted Canyon, proceed down canyon, taking the right fork at any junction. The geology of this area is colorful and invites close examination of the many varieties of rock found uplifted and exposed all along the return route. After a mile the canyon narrows sharply, and hikers are challenged to descend the last several ladders to a lower canyon below. Follow this last 0.75-mile section until you are back to your starting point at the car parking area.

2 Little Painted Canyon Walkabout (see map on page 21)

LENGTH: 4 – 5 miles

HIKING TIME: 3 – 4 hours

ELEVATION GAIN: 300 feet

DIFFICULTY: Easy

SEASON: October to April

INFORMATION: BLM Office, Palm Springs, (760) 251-4800

This hike was designed for hikers who are uncomfortable climbing the ladders through Ladder Canyon that take hikers into the main and largest canyon of the Painted Canyon complex of colorful rock and geological formations. With this hike you will be able to enjoy the Painted Canyon experience without the ladder climbing.

DIRECTIONS

Follow the directions for Hike 1. After you park your car near the turn-around, begin walking into the large canyon just past the sign indicating the end of the road.

You will begin this smaller version of the Painted Canyon hike by walking into the large canyon behind the sign, as indicated in the directions. After 0.25 mile the canyon begins to turn left. Stay to the right and leave the main canyon by hiking into the large canyon area to your right. There is another canyon to

Rock formations near Little Painted Canyon

your left, but by staying right and hiking into the large canyon, you will be on the right track. Do not be fooled into walking into the little side canyons before this turn. Once you veer right, after another 0.25 mile you will again come to a major canyon juncture where the canyon splits into three large canyons, the width of their mouths being 20-30 yards. Again veer to the right, taking the canyon to the far right. I've marked this with a rock cairn just next to the far right wall of the canyon (GPS), but you cannot be sure that this marker will still be there (a large 5x6-foot dirt boulder lies just back of the cairn). Once into this canyon, you are now hiking Little Painted Canyon. As the walls narrow, you will begin seeing spectacular, colorful rock formations. Most of this hike is an easy walkabout through the canyon (stay right in the main canyon except for one obvious left turn).

After 2-plus miles the canyon narrows into a difficult-to-negotiate dry falls. You can proceed farther by retreating 20 yards and then walking left up and over this dry falls or trying the more difficult rock scramble to the right of the dry falls. After another half mile you will probably want to turn back and retrace your route back to your vehicle, staying to the left as you proceed down canyon.

3 *Little and Big Painted Canyon/ Ladders Loop* (see map on page 21)

LENGTH: 5 miles	**SEASON:** October to April
HIKING TIME: 3 hours	**INFORMATION:** BLM Office,
ELEVATION GAIN: 400 feet	Palm Springs, (760) 251-4800
DIFFICULTY: Moderate	

With this loop hike it is possible to experience two parallel "Painted Canyons" and descend the easier set of ladders while avoiding the more demanding first ladders and the scramble to the top ridge of Painted Canyon.

DIRECTIONS   Follow the directions for Hike 2.

After following Little Painted Canyon to the dry falls (2.5 miles from the start), negotiate the dry falls by either retreating 20-30 yards and scrambling up the slope to the left of the falls, or do the more difficult scramble to the right of the dry falls.

From either position, once above the dry falls look up toward the sloping small cliff above you (if you are below the falls looking directly at the dry falls, this cliff is directly to the right and above the falls area). Scramble up this slope where it appears easiest. For some this might mean going up the small gully to the left. Once at the top, depending on from where you scrambled up to the top, walk for a few yards until you notice the trail along the ridge that winds sharply down the other side and into Big Painted Canyon (GPS). Descend into the larger Painted Canyon. At the bottom, looking south down canyon, notice that the darker, more colorful rock begins to be exposed beneath the sandstone and top-covering soil and dry mud. Proceed south down Big Painted Canyon, examining the incredible, colorful, and diverse rock formations along the way. By always staying to your right you will eventually arrive, after 1-1.5 miles, to a rock area highlighted by white, chalky material and dark striped rocks that some refer to as Zebra Rocks. The last ladder of Painted Canyon lies around the corner as the canyon comes to an abrupt narrowing.

Descend the taller of the two ladders, then the smaller one if it is there. If not, just scoot down the last 6-foot rock face. From the bottom of the canyon look back to enjoy the spectacular drop out of Painted Canyon. Continue hiking the canyon along its sandy bottom for another 0.75 mile until you eventually empty out onto the road where your vehicle is parked.

Massive strata rocks dwarf hikers in Painted Canyon

4 Box Canyon's "The Grottos" Cave Hike

LENGTH: 5 miles

HIKING TIME: 3 – 4 hours

ELEVATION GAIN: 300 feet

DIFFICULTY: Easy/moderate

SEASON: October to April

INFORMATION: BLM Office, Palm Springs, (760) 251-4800

At the eastern flank of the Mecca Hills Wilderness area lies Box Canyon. Within this upheaval of sandstone, mud hills, and washes are two "cave" systems formed when an ancient river cut through sandstone mountains. Earthquakes then forced the collapse of parts of these mountain systems to buttress against each other at their tops, leaving the bottom hollow or cavelike in appearance. The hike to the caves offers a stunning view of the Salton Sea and the eastern Santa Rosa Mountains, suggesting Lower Baja California's Sea of Cortez. For this hike, as well as for the 2nd Grotto, bring a good flashlight.

DIRECTIONS Follow the directions for Hike 1 up to the sign indicating Painted Canyon to the left off Hwy. 195. Continue driving on Hwy. 195 exactly 5 miles past the Painted Canyon sign until you can turn right off the road at the tall signpost marked Sheep Hole Oasis. Drive 100 yards to the trailhead located against the mud hill just off the road.

Begin hiking the trail behind the trail sign found at the parking area. The trail leads east up a small water channel for 30 yards before climbing alongside a small hill. Within a few hundred yards you arrive at an overlook of the Salton Sea Basin, before continuing up to the top overlook in another 0.1 mile. From here the trail drops down along a ridge for 0.5 mile. To the left and down in the canyon is a small cluster of palm trees marking Sheep Hole Oasis, a water collection spot for bighorn sheep. The trail then drops down into a canyon where you have two options to access the main canyon, Hidden Springs Canyon.

You can turn right as you reach the canyon floor and hike 100 yards to the main canyon, where you will then turn left and proceed east for 0.6 mile until coming to the narrow entrance accented by an iron gate. Or you can take the "post route" into Hidden Springs Canyon by following the iron posts found in the canyon that you first drop down into as the trail crosses the small wash, climbs a low hill, then drops down into Hidden Springs Canyon; then you'll

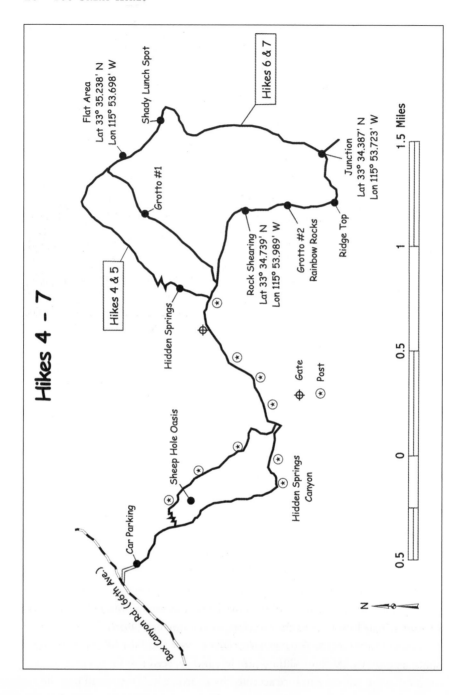

Irrigation runoff continually fills the Salton Sea, making it the largest body of water in California

continue post to post until arriving at the narrow canyon entrance. From here, hike into the increasingly more dramatic canyon for 0.25 mile until coming to a colorful rock formation on your left, a small canyon entrance that leads to Hidden Springs Oasis found 100 yards from the entrance. Note the explosion of colorful rocks on the right side of the canyon as well. After exploring the oasis, return to the main canyon and continue hiking for 100 yards until coming to the first large canyon to your left, marked by a large cluster of trees and bushes. Turn left here and follow the narrowing canyon until it ends in what looks like a rock slide. This marks the entrance to the 1st Grotto cave system.

Carefully climb up the right side of the slide, entering the cave system by dropping down a small ladder after crossing a wooden plank. As you crawl or move about the cave system, be careful not to rise up too quickly, or you might painfully encounter a low-hanging rock! After carefully negotiating the several cave systems found here and exploring up the narrow canyon you exit into, return to your vehicle by following the same route you took back through the Grottos. Be sure not to forget the flashlight! This hike provides some interesting camera shots, so photo enthusiasts will want their cameras as well.

5 Box Canyon First Grotto Loop to Hidden Springs *(see map on page 26)*

LENGTH: 5 miles

HIKING TIME: 3 – 4 hours

ELEVATION GAIN: 400 feet

DIFFICULTY: Moderate

SEASON: October to April

INFORMATION: BLM Office, Palm Springs, (760) 251-4800

DIRECTIONS   Follow the directions for Hike 4.

The Hidden Springs Canyon trail leads to a hiker's oasis, complete with a cool spring and shady palm grove

After negotiating through the cave area, instead of backtracking through the caves, continue hiking the narrowing canyon that exits from the Grottos. After less than 0.5 mile you will notice to your left a steep jeep road coming down into the canyon. Hike up and out this sharp incline. At the top, notice the road turning left. Follow it up another very sharp incline (plenty of quick aerobic exercise in this section) until it tops out on a hill. Take the faint trail to the left and slightly down, (it will begin moving toward the south/southwest). This trail becomes more defined and offers great valley vistas as well as sweeping views of the Salton Sea and its basin.

After 0.75 mile the trail begins to follow a narrowing ridge until it is above Hidden Springs (you can see the palm trees below you). Carefully descend the ridge, a rough bushwhack and scramble, until you are at Hidden Springs Oasis.

This is a great lunch stop. Continue south through the narrow canyon until you empty out into the same large canyon you first hiked up to get to the Grottos. Turn right and proceed down canyon for at least a mile until you notice the large canyon that you entered from earlier in the day. Be especially careful to note this canyon entrance. Upon entering it you will, after 100 yards, come to a large ironwood tree to the left. The trail up the ridge is now visible and will take you back to the vehicle parking area.

6 *Second Grotto/Rainbow Rocks Walkabout* (see map on page 26)

LENGTH: 7 miles	**SEASON:** October to April
HIKING TIME: 5 hours	**INFORMATION:** BLM Office, Palm Springs, (760) 251-4800
ELEVATION GAIN: 800 feet	
DIFFICULTY: Strenuous	

DIRECTIONS Follow the directions for Hike 4.

After coming to the canyon leading into the 1st Grotto, continue past this entrance and instead follow the same canyon you've been hiking in for the last several miles. In another 0.5 to 0.75 mile you will come to a narrowing of the main canyon (Hidden Springs Canyon). Along the way you will notice many colorful formations to your right. Feel free to enter these small side canyons and examine the rainbow display of soil and rock. At the very end of the main canyon, look to your left for a narrow opening (an Alice-in-Wonderland kind of entrance). Crawl into this narrow entrance (flashlights are necessary) and begin negotiating this cave system. After a while you will come to a rock wall that requires careful climbing. Many hikers will feel uncomfortable doing this rock wall and can backtrack

Salton Sea, one of the world's largest inland bodies of saltwater, as viewed from the Grottos

out of the Grotto and return down canyon to the trailhead. If you choose to continue, upon exiting above the wall, notice the rainbow array of rock and soil surrounding you. Take the larger canyon to your right. Feel free to explore the trail system before returning to your vehicle by returning through the 2nd Grotto, following the route you came in on back to your vehicle.

7 Second Grotto/Rainbow Rocks/ Hidden Springs Loop *(see map on page 26)*

LENGTH: 8 miles	**SEASON:** October to April
HIKING TIME: 5 hours	**INFORMATION:** BLM Office,
ELEVATION GAIN: 1,000 feet	Palm Springs, (760) 251-4800
DIFFICULTY: Strenuous	

This hike takes you to the second cave system in the Box Canyon area known as the 2nd Grotto, past colorful rainbow rock formations, to the tops of several mountains for some great vistas, and back to Hidden Springs via a cross-country bushwhack. This is an adventurous hike, physically demanding, with steep uphill and downhill rock scrambles and vertical drop exposures down into deep canyons. In short . . . be prepared, be careful, and be willing to challenge yourself, mentally and physically. This hike is best suited for experienced hikers with land navigation skills.

DIRECTIONS Follow the directions for Hike 4.

After parking at the trailhead, follow the trail just in back of the sign. It begins by hugging a low hill to your right, climbing quickly to the top of one great vista overlook, then another. From the top the trail, head down for 0.5 mile along a ridge offering you spectacular views of the lower Salton Sea Basin, the Santa Rosa Mountains to the south, and the Box Canyon foothills. Note the palm trees down in the canyon to your left. This marks the spot for Sheep Hole Oasis, a small opening in the ground where water is available most of the year for bighorn sheep.

From the ridge the trail eventually drops down into a canyon. As a variation on other hikes into Hidden Springs Canyon and eventually to the 2nd Grotto (GPS), follow the iron posts in the wash as they lead you up to a small hill overlook and then down into Hidden Springs Canyon. This "post route" can now be

Colorful rainbow rock formations give this area its name

simply negotiated by following the posts as they lead through the main canyon to where the iron gate partially crosses the canyon and the canyon narrows.

Note the rock formations on either side of the canyon, especially the ones on the left where the softer base rock has eroded, allowing the harder stone it supports to break and fall down the hillside. After passing the gate and hiking for 0.25 mile, observe the two sentinel-like dark purple rocks guarding a narrow opening to the left. This marks the entrance to Hidden Springs Oasis, from which you will exit on your return.

Along the route of the next half mile and to your right, you will enjoy a series of colorful "rainbow rock formations," which you can examine by walking a few yards off the main canyon. Along the same route you will also come to a rock formation on your right where uplift and possible severe rock shearing forces have broken off pieces of rock in a dramatic fashion (GPS).

As the canyon ends in an intensifying explosion of color, take the entrance to the left into the 2nd Grotto. You begin this part of the hike by crawling through the small opening into a series of chambers. You must negotiate narrow rock blockages until coming to "the wall," a 12-foot vertical rise that demands careful rock climbing. Once at the top you are "through" the 2nd Grotto. Follow the canyon for 30 yards until you turn right at the first opportunity. This narrow canyon leads slowly upward, in a stair-step fashion. When you come to the big boulder sitting on the ledge to your right, stay left in the still-narrow canyon, then right at the next junction, hiking up toward an ocotillo on the upper right ridge above you. In a few yards, veer left past the nearby ocotillo, then left of the large rocky upthrust, aiming for the large, shiplike rock above you to your left.

Climb up the 4-foot-high ridge to your left, then make for the top of the mountain by scrambling up its steep sides until you reach the top (40 yards).

At the top, turn left, being especially careful of the exposure and narrow trail conditions. Enjoy the views, but not while you are hiking! Stop first, then take in the magnificent scenery. After about 150 yards, veer right, heading toward the three rock cairns atop the mountain east of you. After another 100 yards you will come to the last ridge junction (GPS). Do not take the trail to the cairns. Instead, follow the steep trail leading sharply down on the left, a trail that demands extreme caution because of loose rock and steep drops. After another 75 yards, veer left and then right to the faint trail that summits the steep hill due north. From atop this hill, head north by slowly and carefully stair-stepping your way down the north face of the hill until coming to a small saddle. Drop down left into a wash then head for the next steep hill to the northwest, following the jeep trail up to the top.

By now you're wondering what possessed you to ever consider taking this hike in the first place . . . but persevere, your land navigation skills will see you safely home!

From the top of this next hill, follow the jeep road down its steep north face, eventually coming out into a large wash accented by many palo verde trees— the trees with the green bark. Continue left down the wash for 0.25 mile until coming to a large palo verde that makes a shady lunch/snack stop. Stay in the wash for another 0.25 to 0.5 mile until you see a large boulder, to the right of which a jeep trail climbs steeply out. If you continue to follow the wash, it quickly becomes a narrow canyon leading directly into the 1st Grotto.

After taking the steep jeep trail out of the wash, you summit onto a flat area. Look left and then follow the jeep trail that drops down and then quickly up onto another steep hill climb. Just a few yards from the top look for a faint trail veering left. This bighorn sheep trail leads you up to the hilltop and almost joins the jeep road to your right. Stay on the narrow trail as it turns left and then south away from the jeep road, following a ridge for the next 0.5 mile and offering beautiful vista views of the Salton Sea and Rainbow Canyon/Rocks to the left.

The trail will narrow to a steep ridge just above Hidden Springs Oasis. Take it down, to the left, to the oasis, then out the narrow canyon, where you will negotiate more rock obstacles. Once back in the main canyon, follow the post route until it climbs the first hill. The trail up and to your right will take you down into the wash, where you turn right to access Sheep Hole Oasis, about 0.5 mile up canyon. One final steep trail left of the second set of palm trees leads you to the high ridge trail you first came in on. At the top, turn right and follow the trail back to your parked vehicle.

This hike is demanding, requires an adventurous attitude, land navigation skills, and physical stamina. It rewards the hiker with a sense of accomplishment, the fun challenges of following a bushwhack route, plenty of awesome vista views of the Salton Sea Basin and Rainbow Canyon/Rocks area, and a generous scattering of magnificent quartz specimens. This hike is best done on a sunny day, early in the morning, and before the temperature reaches into the 80s.

Coachella Preserve
Hikes 8 – 10

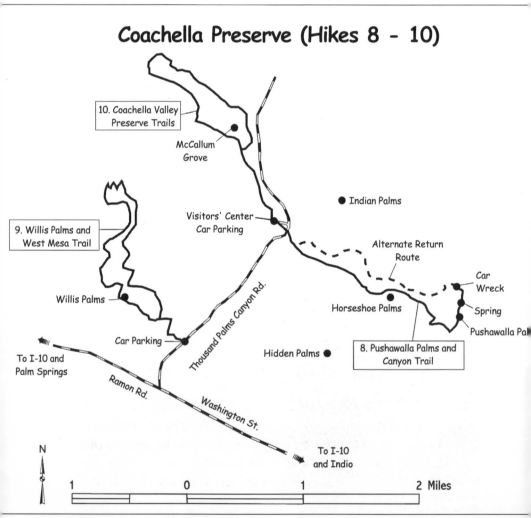

Coachella Preserve (Hikes 8 - 10)

10. Coachella Valley Preserve Trails

McCallum Grove

● Indian Palms

Visitors' Center Car Parking

9. Willis Palms and West Mesa Trail

Alternate Return Route

Car Wreck

Willis Palms

Horseshoe Palms

Spring

Pushawalla Pa

Car Parking

Thousand Palms Canyon Rd.

Hidden Palms ●

8. Pushawalla Palms and Canyon Trail

To I-10 and Palm Springs

Ramon Rd.

Washington St.

To I-10 and Indio

N

1   0   1   2 Miles

8

Pushawalla Palms and Canyon Trail *(see map on page 34)*

LENGTH: 6 miles

HIKING TIME: 4 hours

ELEVATION GAIN: 300 feet

DIFFICULTY: Easy

SEASON: October to April

INFORMATION: Coachella Valley Preserve, Thousand Palms (760) 343-1234

The 13,000-acre Coachella Valley Preserve is a lush concentration of California fan palms, rising miraculously in the alluvial gravel and sand deposits from the Little San Bernardino Mountains and Indio Hills. The San Andreas Fault encourages water to seep up to the surface. Here seeds of the fan palm, nourished by this once subterranean water, have grown into more than 1,200 palms. A system of trails has been built to assist the visitor in seeing the wondrous effects of water and plant life surrounded by desert sands, low hills, and gentle canyons.

DIRECTIONS   To reach the preserve, drive on I-10 to Washington Street exit, and drive left (north) for 5 miles, reaching Thousand Palms Canyon Road. Turn right and park in the preserve, located 2 miles after the turn.

To begin the Pushawalla Palms Trail, head southeast from the parking lot toward the rocky bluff across the road.

A long grove of palms grows in the narrow Pushawalla Canyon

Once up the hill you will be atop Bee-Rock Mesa. A trail heads to the left and takes you above Horseshoe Palms and then on into Pushawalla Palms Canyon. Or you can hike in a more southeast direction to arrive at the canyon before dropping down to explore the full length of the oasis. Pushawalla Palms represents a long grove of palms growing in the narrow Pushawalla Canyon. There is a small stream running during the winter if rains have been plentiful. Unless it is done in early morning, anytime after March may be too hot for the unseasoned desert visitor to take this hike.

9 *Willis Palms and West Mesa Trail*

(see map on page 34)

LENGTH: 3 miles

HIKING TIME: 2 hours

ELEVATION GAIN: 300 feet

DIFFICULTY: Easy

SEASON: October to April

INFORMATION: Coachella Valley Preserve, Thousand Palms (760) 343-1234

This is another Coachella Valley Preserve hike that takes you to a grove of California fan palms situated on the San Andreas Fault and offers you expansive views of the western half of the Coachella Valley. While rated an easy hike, there is a climb up a short but steep cliff, and hikers new to the desert should be aware of warmer springtime temperatures.

DIRECTIONS

To reach the trailhead, follow Washington Street north from I-10, as given in the directions for Hike 8. After turning right at Thousand Palms Canyon Road, look to your left at the low rise of hills. The trail begins after turning onto this road and is found to your left.

The trail starts west for 0.25 mile and then heads north up a sandy wash. Stay right in the wash, follow the trail for another mile, then up the side of the cliff. You will see some great views of the western Coachella Valley. Continue following the trail as it turns south and back to your starting position. Always take plenty of cool water even on a desert hike as short as this.

A relatively easy hike, this trail offers great views of the western Coachella Valley Preserve

10 *Coachella Valley Preserve Trails*

(see map on page 34)

LENGTH: 6 miles

HIKING TIME: 5 hours

ELEVATION GAIN: 100 feet

DIFFICULTY: Easy

SEASON: October to April

INFORMATION: Coachella Valley Preserve, Thousand Palms (760) 343-1234

The Coachella Valley Preserve is a great place to walk trails that are less demanding yet offer a real desert and oasis experience. The preserve is truly an island in the desert, with generous plant and bird life surrounded by small desert canyons, hills, washes, and mesas.

DIRECTIONS

The preserve is reached by exiting from I-10 onto Washington Street, traveling north for 5 miles. Turn right at Thousand Palms Road for 2 miles until you see the lush vegetation on your left and the sign indicating the entrance.

There are several easy trails on the preserve, ranging from less than 0.25 mile to 1, 1.4, and 3 miles. The elevation gain is less than 100 feet but the hikes do cover sandy trails—especially the Wash Trail—and tend to slow the hike into a gentle walk.

The Coachella Valley Preserve is indeed a place to walk, enjoy scenes of rich plant and bird life, and capture the essence of a desert oasis. It is open from sunrise to sunset.

Desert verbena in spring bloom

Desert Cities
Hikes 11 – 17

Trailhead Locations in Desert Cities
(Hikes 11 - 17)

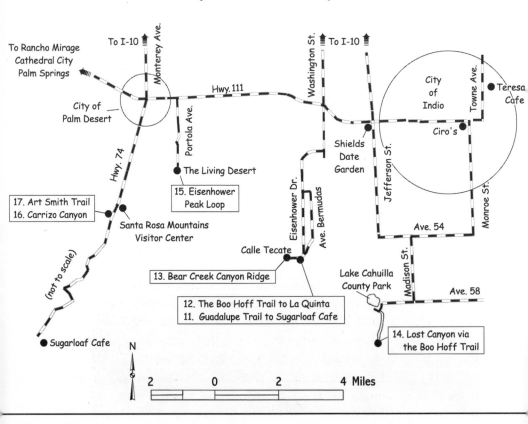

To Rancho Mirage
Cathedral City
Palm Springs

To I-10

Monterey Ave.

Washington St.

To I-10

City
of
Indio

Towne Ave.

Teresa
Cafe

Hwy. 111

City of
Palm Desert

Portola Ave.

Ciro's

Hwy. 74

Shields
Date
Garden

Jefferson St.

The Living Desert

15. Eisenhower
Peak Loop

Eisenhower Dr.

Ave. Bermudas

Monroe St.

17. Art Smith Trail
16. Carrizo Canyon

Santa Rosa Mountains
Visitor Center

Ave. 54

Calle Tecate

13. Bear Creek Canyon Ridge

Madison St.

Lake Cahuilla
County Park

Ave. 58

(not to scale)

12. The Boo Hoff Trail to La Quinta
11. Guadalupe Trail to Sugarloaf Cafe

Sugarloaf Cafe

14. Lost Canyon via
the Boo Hoff Trail

N

2   0   2   4 Miles

11   *Guadalupe Trail to Sugarloaf Cafe*

LENGTH: 15 miles

HIKING TIME: 8 hours

ELEVATION GAIN: 5,000 feet

DIFFICULTY: Very strenuous

SEASON: October to April

INFORMATION: BLM Office, Palm Springs, (760) 251-4800

While not commonly found on most hiking maps, the Guadalupe Trail to Sugarloaf Cafe is one of the premier strenuous wilderness hikes in the Santa Rosa Mountains. This hike requires a shuttle, with cars parked at Sugarloaf Cafe on Hwy. 74, 14 miles up the road from Palm Desert, and at the Boo Hoff/La Quinta trailhead. The climb up the northeast flank of Martinez Mountain—or at least it's close enough to be considered Martinez Mountain—gives hikers incredible vistas of the entire lower Coachella Valley and Salton Sea Basin. Eventually the trail penetrates the upper reaches of the Santa Rosa Wilderness and joins with the Cactus Spring Trail for the trek back through Horsethief Creek.

DIRECTIONS

To reach the trailhead, take Hwy. 111 to La Quinta at Washington Street. Turn south onto Washington Street (right, if you are going east on Hwy. 111 from Palm Desert). After several miles, turn right onto Eisenhower Street (stoplight) and continue several more miles until Eisenhower dead-ends at Avenida Bermudas. Turn right and go for 0.3 mile until you see Avenida Ramirez on your right. Turn left off the road and into the dirt parking lot.

Start the hike by heading south by southeast across the open dirt flatlands, following the dirt path. After 0.25 mile you will reach the drop-off from the flat area, going down and around some metal posts and into a wash. Follow the trail and wash, first going right and then left (south), heading past some junky remains of trash. This dirt path heads south toward the opening between two low hills. After 0.5 mile the trail climbs right and up onto a small ridge above the canyon you've been hiking in. Follow the trail above the ridge, as it soon veers down and into the small canyon to your right. Stay right for another 0.25 mile and you will soon come to a metal sign which reads "Boo Hoff Trail."

From here, the hike is part of the Boo Hoff Trail, as it climbs steeply up the mountainside. About 3 miles up on your right is a small rock cairn, the "official" start of the Guadalupe Trail. This is actually an old Indian trail, which

Winter runoff often forms temporary waterfalls

travels through the Guadalupe Canyon and along the rim of Devil's Canyon. The trail looks onto steep, granite sanctuaries for bighorn sheep. Ahead of you as you climb south up this steep, rocky, and sometimes faint trail, will be a tepee-type peak.

Farther up the trail, 4 miles from the parked vehicles, is an Indian flat area (tepee-type peak is now 50 feet east), where pottery pieces might be found. As the trail winds relentlessly up the mountains, you will reach a top area where pine and juniper begin to accent the slopes. As you enter the level mountainous area, you will come upon an old cowboy camp, where the remains of stoves, iron implements, tin cans, etc., can be found strewn over a wide area. The trail pushes back from here into a dense canyon thicket, where a stream sometimes flows during wet winters. Eventually the trail breaks out into a widening wash, which you will favor as it veers slowly to the right. In a short time you will come to your first signpost, indicating that your trail is joining with the Cactus Spring Trail. Follow this trail right (west) for 2 miles to Horsethief Creek and another 2.5 miles to the Cactus Spring Trailhead. From here you can follow the jeep road to Sugarloaf Cafe just up the hill, along Hwy. 74. As demanding as this trail is, it is worth all the effort, but it is most safely done with someone knowing the way.

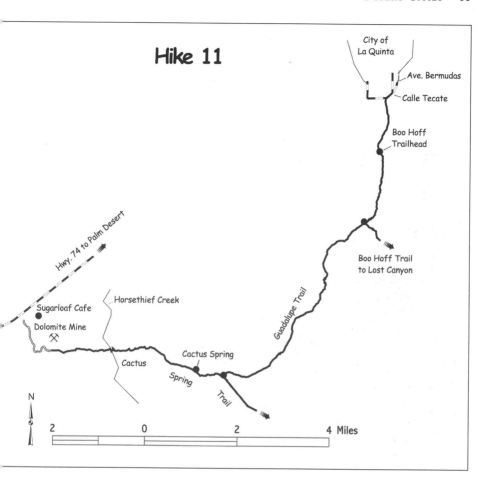

Hike 11

City of
La Quinta

Ave. Bermudas

Calle Tecate

Boo Hoff
Trailhead

Boo Hoff Trail
to Lost Canyon

Hwy. 74 to Palm Desert

Horsethief Creek

Sugarloaf Cafe

Dolomite Mine

Guadalupe Trail

Cactus Spring

Cactus

Spring

Trail

N

2   0   2   4 Miles

12 *The Boo Hoff Trail to La Quinta*

LENGTH: 12 miles

HIKING TIME: 6 – 7 hours

ELEVATION GAIN: 2,000 feet

DIFFICULTY: Strenuous

SEASON: October to April

INFORMATION: BLM Office, Palm Springs, (760) 251-4800

The Boo Hoff Trail takes the hiker deep into the Santa Rosa Mountains along the north drainage of Martinez Mountain, with wide, impressive vistas of the Salton Sea Basin. This interior trail leads into the wilderness areas where hikers find it difficult to believe that just over the hill is the sprawling Coachella Valley and the city of La Quinta. Along the way the trail treats you to wild desert mountains, solitude and, if you are lucky, some of the bighorn sheep, which live in the Santa Rosa Wilderness.

DIRECTIONS   Follow the directions for Hike 14, until you reach the trail sign for the Boo Hoff Trail.

Continue up the Boo Hoff Trail for the better part of 2 miles until the canyon drops down into the wash just past the sprawl of cholla cacti. Continue up the trail, as it climbs up and out of the wash. You will gradually climb 2 more miles. Along the way are numerous side canyons, dry falls, and washes that are typical of the Santa Rosa Wilderness. Following a wet winter, sometime between mid-March and mid-April, you will see rivers of flowers flowing from the canyon sides along the trail. These can be spectacular but must have enough water to

really grow profusely. (Be sure to start early on the trail, as it gets hot this time of year.)

At the western end of the Boo Hoff Trail, you will find yourself above La Quinta. From here you can turn around and head east, retracing the same route. Some hikers make a shuttle hike out of the Boo Hoff Trail by following the wash/jeep road down to the street. This way, the hike is about 8-9 miles one way. The trail was affectionately named for Mr. Boo Hoff, a leading figure with the equestrian group, The Desert Trail Riders.

Hikers navigate the Boo Hoff Trail

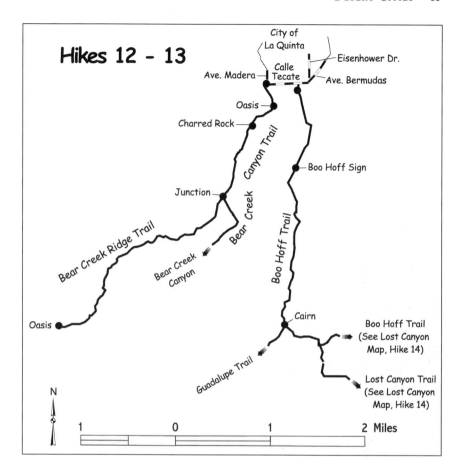

Hikes 12 - 13

City of La Quinta

Eisenhower Dr.

Calle Tecate

Ave. Madera

Ave. Bermudas

Oasis

Charred Rock

Bear Creek Canyon Trail

Boo Hoff Sign

Junction

Bear Creek Ridge Trail

Bear Creek Canyon

Boo Hoff Trail

Oasis

Cairn

Boo Hoff Trail (See Lost Canyon Map, Hike 14)

Guadalupe Trail

Lost Canyon Trail (See Lost Canyon Map, Hike 14)

N

1   0   1   2 Miles

13 *Bear Creek Canyon Ridge*

LENGTH: 8 miles

HIKING TIME: 5 hours

ELEVATION GAIN: 2,000 feet

DIFFICULTY: Strenuous

SEASON: October to April

INFORMATION: BLM Office, Palm Springs, (760) 251-4800

This hike is one of the many canyon hikes found along the foothills of the Santa Rosa Mountains. These mountains form the southern boundary of the Coachella Valley, with Martinez Mountain dominating the southeast portion of this range. Bear Creek Canyon flows north as a major drainage from Martinez Mountain, towards the sleepy city of La Quinta. The ridge affords expansive views of not only the city, but also, in a single sweep of the eyes, both the Salton Sea and the distant, often snow-capped San Jacinto and San Gorgonio peaks.

DIRECTIONS

To reach the trailhead, take Hwy. 111 to La Quinta and turn right (south) at Washington Street into La Quinta. Continue to Eisenhower Drive, turn right, and follow Eisenhower until it ends at the end of town at Avenida Bermudas. Turn right, noting that Avenida Bermudas becomes Calle Tecate. Park where Calle Tecate meets Avenida Madero. Looking to the south you will see broad, sandy flatlands bordered by low foothills to the right.

Rock scrambling through the Santa Rosa Mountains

Begin walking south on the dirt path that makes its way between a low ridge of foothills and a palm oasis left of the trail. The trail then veers to the right before being blocked by some boulders, and then drops into a wide wash.

Once you're in the wash, turn south (left) and favor the left for about a 20-minute walk. Chuparosa, with its colorful red and orange blossoms, is abundant, especially from February to April. As the canyon narrows, look for the small, sharply defined canyon to your right that shows charred rock from campers' use. Just past this canyon, at the palo verde tree, is the beginning of Bear Creek Canyon Ridge Trail.

For the first 0.5 mile, stay on the established trail, being careful of false side trails, which are often blocked by rocks. As you climb back into the massive canyon network, you can feel a wild, distant land, void of any human influence. After 1.5 miles you will begin to rapidly ascend the ridge, surrounded by ocotillo that dominate the landscape. Down to your left is the massive rocky canyon of Bear Creek, offering a good water flow during bountiful, wet winters.

After 2 miles, hikers will find themselves on a plateau from which they can see the mountain ranges surrounding the Coachella Valley, and the Salton Sea to the east. A lacework of canyons flowing from the Santa Rosas surround the trail in all directions. As you continue up the trail, the views to the north allow you to peek into Joshua Tree National Park. Still farther up, the hiker is treated to hidden valleys deep in the interior mountains and the culmination of a massive verdant oasis tucked into the fold of a canyon. Here you are over 4 miles from the trailhead. You can choose to lunch here or continue exploring to see what lies over the next ridge. There are no trails beyond the oasis, but any wash will lead you into either dry or flowing waterfalls, depending on how wet the winter has been.

14 *Lost Canyon via the Boo Hoff Trail*

LENGTH: 10 miles

HIKING TIME: 5 hours

ELEVATION GAIN: 1,500 feet

DIFFICULTY: Strenuous

SEASON: October to April

INFORMATION: BLM Office, Palm Springs, (760) 251-4800

Hikers find the breathtaking views at Lost Canyon are well worth the effort

Of the many canyon hikes found in the foothills of the Santa Rosa Mountains, the Lost Canyon hike offers some of the most diversified terrain and breathtaking views. For the entire hike the massive, imposing form of Martinez Mountain looms above the hiker's southern view. During a rainy winter, the north face of the mountain is streaked with many rivulet-type waterfalls. These serve to accent the canyons emerging from the mountainside and feed the vegetation trapped in washes. Although plant life is sparse, cholla and barrel cacti along with ocotillo are abundantly dispersed throughout the length of the hike.

DIRECTIONS

Lost Canyon is reached by driving several miles east past the city of La Quinta on Hwy. 111, turning right onto Jefferson Street, and proceeding until you reach the PGA West Golf Club. Turn left at PGA West (Avenue 54), right at the next stop sign (Madison Street), and right again at Avenue 58, following the signs to Lake Cahuilla County Park. Near the lake the road dips after a rise and splits to the left and right. If you do not have a 4WD vehicle, park in the land area formed between the road split. If you can drive farther, continue to the left until you approach the guarded gate to the Quarry Golf Club, and take a sharp left into the desert and onto a recognizable jeep road. Follow this east for several hundred yards, then south along the low foothills until you reach the dike. Drive over the dike, following the jeep trail for 1 mile. Park where there is a stone cairn to the right of the trail. Walk toward the mountain.

As the trail narrows, bear to the right. You can see that you are coming up to a rather large canyon against the mountains. Look to the right for a black metal sign which marks the beginning of the Boo Hoff Trail. Take this trail into the high foothills. As the wilderness canyons of the Santa Rosa Mountains impress you with dry and sometimes wet waterfalls along the north face of Martinez Mountain, you will feel you are truly away from it all.

As you ascend, look south. You will be following a large canyon, which at this point in the hike begins to draw closer. After 1.5 miles on the Boo Hoff Trail you will begin to drop down into a thickly vegetated wash, after passing through an extensive stand of cholla cacti. Although the trail continues on the hillside past the wash, turn left into the wash and begin traveling down canyon. Stay to the right as you climb down several dry waterfalls until you come to the spectacular canyon drop that spills into Lost Canyon. Most hikers can negotiate this 150-foot drop without a rope. Stay to the left as you crawl down the rockfalls and onto the trail above it. Continue bearing left and descend down into the canyon. Be especially careful of loose gravel and rock. With its view of the Salton Sea framed by the slopes of Lost Canyon, this section looks awesome and might appear impassable. But children—with careful adults there to help— have done this section without incident, so it's as safe as the hiker is.

Take the canyon left for 0.5 mile until you reach another large dry falls. The trail can be found 15 to 20 yards before you reach the falls, and up on the hillside to your right. Here you will drop down into your final canyon. To the right, at 200 yards, is a waterfall, generously flowing after a good rainfall. After seeing this last waterfall, turn back and continue down canyon for 0.5 mile until you see the Boo Hoff Trail marker to your left. From here it's a simple matter of following the wash back to your vehicle.

The Lost Canyon hike is impressive to desert visitors for its cacti, soaring canyons, impressive views, and most of all that unforgettable descent down the large dry falls that upon first glance leaves some hikers with a feeling of "no way!"

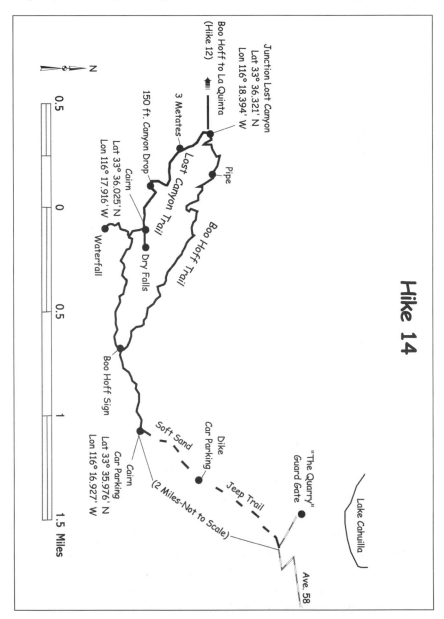

15   *Eisenhower Peak Loop*

LENGTH: 6 miles

HIKING TIME: 4 hours

ELEVATION GAIN: 700 feet

DIFFICULTY: Moderate

SEASON: October to April

INFORMATION: The Living Desert, Palm Desert (760) 346-5694

The Living Desert is a visitor's mecca for those wishing to learn more about the flora and fauna of the Coachella Valley. This preserve has grown to include its own wildlife zoo. You will find walking paths that highlight varieties of plant and animal life found in the local desert. As you would expect, there is also a major hiking trail within the grounds that takes you up toward Eisenhower Peak, whose 1,952-foot elevation corresponds perfectly to his election year! The trail is a good representation of desert terrain and makes a perfect beginning to your Living Desert tour.

DIRECTIONS   To reach the trailhead, turn south onto Portola Avenue from Hwy. 111 in Palm Desert. After 2 miles you will see the entrance to the Living Desert on your left. From the main entrance, turn right and follow the sidewalk and signs to the wilderness loop. Many docents are available to help direct you. Pick up a plant and tree guide as you leave the main building, as the plant life is well marked along the trail.

After you've walked 0.75 mile to the end of the inner loop, then 0.75 mile to the Quail Guzzler, the canyon leg starts. This is very rugged terrain, necessitating wash-walking and boulder-hopping. At the 0.75-mile marker post, you will begin to climb a very defined trail heading first east and then north to the picnic tables. Eisenhower Mountain is directly on the right but you must bushwhack to the top, as there is no defined trail. The view from the top gives you a fabulous look at the whole of the Coachella Valley. After leaving the tables and heading down the ridge leg, you are treated to stunning glimpses of the estate homes of Eldorado and Vintage Country Clubs. Signs along the way highlight the history of both the palm trees and the trail itself. This section is an easy 1.5-mile meander back to the patio, the bookstore, and a well-deserved snack in the main buildings. In warmer months be sure to bring 2 quarts of a cool drink to quench the desert thirst.

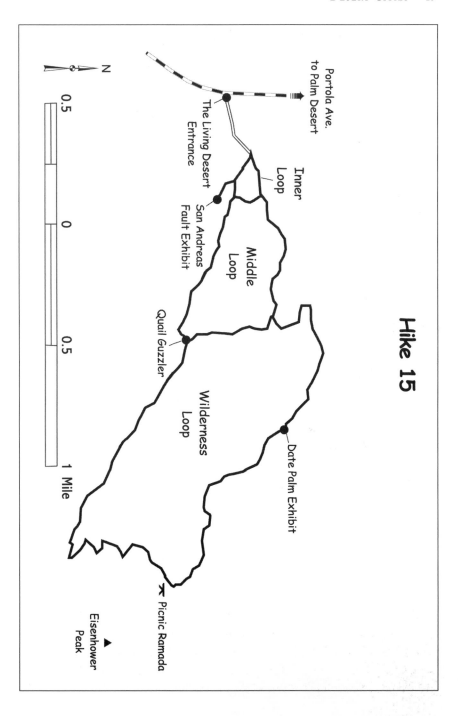

Hike 15

Portola Ave.
to Palm Desert

The Living Desert
Entrance

Inner
Loop

San Andreas
Fault Exhibit

Middle
Loop

Quail Guzzler

Wilderness
Loop

Date Palm Exhibit

Picnic Ramada

Eisenhower
Peak

N

0.5   0   0.5   1 Mile

16 *Carrizo Canyon*

LENGTH: 4 – 6 miles

HIKING TIME: 3 – 4 hours

ELEVATION GAIN: 500 feet

DIFFICULTY: Moderate

SEASON: October to April

INFORMATION: BLM Office, Palm Springs, (760) 251-4800

This is another Santa Rosa Mountain trail that exposes the hiker to canyon hiking. Most of this hike takes place in the canyon and is highlighted by a series of dry or wet waterfalls, depending on the amount of rainfall. In a wet season the hiker is treated to lush vegetation that hardly suggests the presence of the surrounding harsh desert, minutes from the narrow confines of the canyon interior.

DIRECTIONS

To get to Carrizo Canyon, turn south from Hwy. 111 in Palm Desert onto Hwy. 74. After about 4 miles the highway begins to turn up the mountains just past the Bighorn Development to your right. You can park in the parking lot on the right side of the road designated Art Smith Trailhead, 0.25 mile past the Santa Rosa Wilderness Area sign.

Rocks and vegetation line the canyon bottom

Drop down into the wash, or south of where you park, and hike up the wash as it veers to the left and on into Carrizo Canyon. It can be pleasantly cool here, even in the warmer spring months, but it is always wise to carry at least 2 quarts of a cool drink—no matter how cool the canyon is.

Continue along the canyon floor until you reach the first large falls, and climb above it by scrambling up the right side. Be careful of wet rock or algae, and make sure your footholds are secure. You can continue up this canyon's many falls, but be aware that this can be tiring. This is a great short hike that gives the hiker a

sense of adventure, being "on the edge" enough to keep your attention, while
showing the rocky innards of a typical desert canyon. As the trail continues
up the side of the mountain it becomes more of a rock scramble and should
be attempted only by hikers comfortable with this kind of combination
hiking/scrambling.

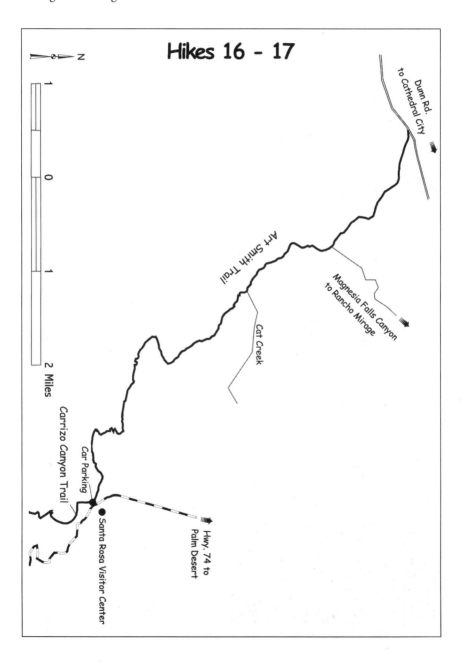

Hikes 16 - 17

17 *Art Smith Trail*

(see map on page 51)

LENGTH: 16 miles

HIKING TIME: 8 hours

ELEVATION GAIN: 1,200 feet

DIFFICULTY: Strenuous

SEASON: October to April

INFORMATION: BLM Office, Palm Springs, (760) 251-4800

This hike is a real treat for the hiker who enjoys a full day's journey without excessive elevation gains. The Art Smith Trail serves as a major link between the Palm Desert portion of the Santa Rosa Mountains and Palm Canyon's network of trails, including the Murray Peak area south of Cathedral City. This day hike allows you to penetrate the mountains while resting along the way in the several palm oases that accent the trail.

DIRECTIONS To reach the trailhead, turn south from Hwy. 111 in Palm Desert onto Hwy. 74. After 4 miles, park at the Santa Rosa Mountains Visitor's Center or across the street at the paved Art Smith Trailhead parking lot.

Head west on the trail that begins next to the Art Smith Trailhead parking lot. This trail skirts the nearby mountain, passes through and above a wash, and after less than a half mile leads into a major wash highlighted by boulders and rocks exposed after a flash flood. Continue until you reach the first major canyon that you can turn right into. Follow the trail for 50 yards until you reach an obvious, developed trail heading north along the hillside. After ⅛ mile you will come to the black metal sign designating the Art Smith Trail.

The trail winds steeply up the mountain for 0.5 mile until leveling out. From here you can see the Bighorn Development below. The trail takes you through several palm oases for the next 2 miles. During March and April, this section of the trail is abundant with plant life, barrel cacti, and other colorful wildflowers and cacti in bloom . . . a real contrast to the stark look in autumn.

By the third mile you are hiking beneath the flat-topped Haystack Mountain facing due south. As you continue, the cities of the valley floor look up from the north, but at times the trail takes you into sheltered areas where no civilization is apparent. After almost 5 miles, the trail crosses the upper reaches of Magnesia Canyon, a palm-filled canyon that makes a sheltered lunch stop. Feel free to explore down the canyon before continuing to the western end of the trail at Dunn Road.

Palm Desert as viewed from the Art Smith Trail

Palm Springs and Indian Canyons

Hikes 18 – 32

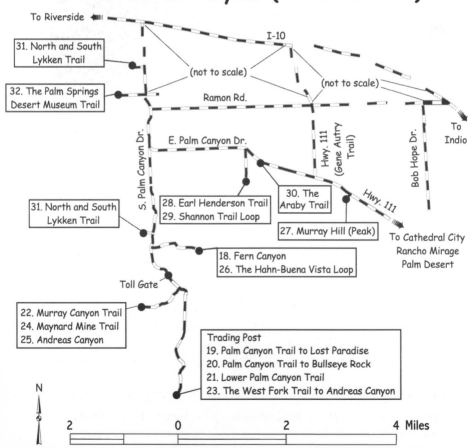

Trailhead Locations in Palm Springs and Indian Canyons (Hikes 18 - 32)

To Riverside

I-10

31. North and South Lykken Trail

(not to scale)

(not to scale)

32. The Palm Springs Desert Museum Trail

Ramon Rd.

To Indio

S. Palm Canyon Dr.

E. Palm Canyon Dr.

Hwy. 111 (Gene Autry Trail)

Bob Hope Dr.

31. North and South Lykken Trail

28. Earl Henderson Trail
29. Shannon Trail Loop

30. The Araby Trail

Hwy. 111

27. Murray Hill (Peak)

To Cathedral City
Rancho Mirage
Palm Desert

18. Fern Canyon
26. The Hahn-Buena Vista Loop

Toll Gate

22. Murray Canyon Trail
24. Maynard Mine Trail
25. Andreas Canyon

Trading Post
19. Palm Canyon Trail to Lost Paradise
20. Palm Canyon Trail to Bullseye Rock
21. Lower Palm Canyon Trail
23. The West Fork Trail to Andreas Canyon

N

2   0   2   4 Miles

18 *Fern Canyon*

LENGTH: 10 miles

HIKING TIME: 5 hours

ELEVATION GAIN: 1,200 feet

DIFFICULTY: Strenuous

SEASON: October to April

INFORMATION: BLM Office, Palm Springs, (760) 251-4800

Palm Canyon Trail rewards the dedicated hiker with lush palm oases along the trail

Fern Canyon offers the hiker the surprise find of a generous outgrowth of ferns growing in a cactus-filled desert! The hike allows you great views of the South Palm Canyon near Hermit's Bench (the Indian Trading Post) and good vistas of Palm Springs and the nearby San Jacinto Mountains and canyons.

DIRECTIONS

This hike begins by taking Hwy. 111 into Palm Springs and then turning onto South Palm Canyon Drive to Bogert Trail, heading east over Palm Canyon Wash. Turn left on Barona Road. The trailhead begins east of the road barricade.

Follow the trail up along a barbed wire fence, 50 yards to the trail signs "1966 DV Garstin & Earl Henderson." Proceed right, up the Garstin Trail and many switchbacks for 2 miles to the next signpost marking the Wildhorse/Berns/Shannon/Garstin/Palm Canyon trails. Go right at this signpost, continuing on the Garstin Trail. Shortly you will come to a "Y" intersection; keep right. Continue for another mile to the trailhead sign for Fern Canyon/Vandeventer/Hahn–Buena Vista/Art Smith/Palm Canyon. Continue walking up the ridge as you enjoy the views of Cathedral City to the north and South Palm Canyon to the south. Hike 0.75 mile until reaching a "Y" intersection and the Clara Burgess Trailhead. Stay right (south), hiking onto a plateau/wash. In spring this area is alive with blossoms from cacti, encelia, scrub brush . . . a carpet of color!

Follow the gently sloping wash down to where a second wash joins from the north (left). Proceed right toward Palm Canyon. Eventually you are rewarded with a lush palm oasis, where a huge boulder covered with dripping water and gorgeous ferns is located. From here you can either backtrack or continue into Palm Canyon and the Indian Trading Post if water levels permit.

A shorter way into Fern Canyon is to drive into Palm Canyon all the way to the trading post, which is less than 3 miles from Fern Canyon. Hike down the walkway into Palm Canyon, then turn left and hike along the stream. Cross over the stream after 0.5 mile and follow the trail up the side canyon to Fern Canyon.

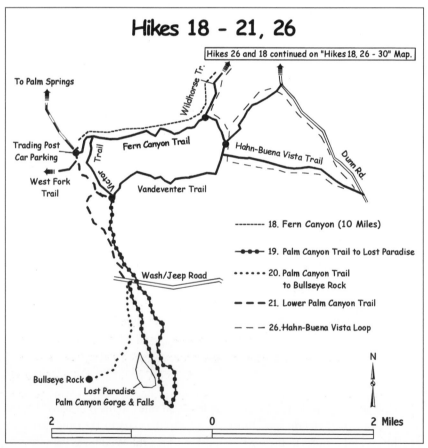

Hikes 18 - 21, 26

Hikes 26 and 18 continued on "Hikes 18, 26 - 30" Map.

To Palm Springs

Wildhorse Tr.

Trading Post
Car Parking

Victor Trail

Fern Canyon Trail

Hahn-Buena Vista Trail

Dunn Rd.

West Fork
Trail

Vandeventer Trail

-------- 18. Fern Canyon (10 Miles)

-●-●-● 19. Palm Canyon Trail to Lost Paradise

• • • • • 20. Palm Canyon Trail
          to Bullseye Rock

Wash/Jeep Road

— — — 21. Lower Palm Canyon Trail

– – – 26. Hahn-Buena Vista Loop

N

Bullseye Rock ●
        Lost Paradise
Palm Canyon Gorge & Falls

2   0   2 Miles

19 *Palm Canyon Trail to Lost Paradise*

LENGTH: 8 miles

HIKING TIME: 5 hours

ELEVATION GAIN: 1,000 feet

DIFFICULTY: Moderate

SEASON: October to April

INFORMATION: BLM Office, Palm Springs, (760) 251-4800

Hikers often refer to the destination of this hike as "Lost Paradise"—for good reason. This trail takes you through the lush junglelike river bottom of Palm Canyon, out onto backcountry high desert plateaus where the entire horizon seems to open up. Looking 14 miles south toward the distant Santa Rosa Mountains, the trail is surrounded by the soaring San Jacintos, which thrust up dramatically from the canyon floor. Stunning views of the desert and Palm Springs will appear to your rear, followed by a series of magnificent plunging cliffs, waterfalls, and exotic pools fed by clear, shimmering ribbons of water racing through the rock gorges. What are we waiting for? Let's go!

DIRECTIONS   Begin this hike by reaching Palm Canyon in the Agua Caliente Indian Canyons south of Palm Springs, as described in Hike 21.

As you pass the right fork of Palm Canyon, veer left and follow the streambed and trail for another 0.5 mile until you reach the marker indicating that the trail crosses the stream and climbs up the south bank and the ridge above. Head south along this trail. Very soon the climb takes you out into the open country where the full, magnificent beauty of these canyons can be appreciated. The trail stays on a high plateau, with some occasional glimpses into small adjacent canyons. After 2 miles of hiking you will reach a wide dirt wash/jeep road. Take the trail straight ahead, rather than following the wash to the left. You will eventually arrive at a place where the trail melts away into the sandy rock, but is still faintly visible on the slowly climbing rise above the canyon to your right. For this reason it is best to travel here with someone knowledgeable of these parts, for example, the Coachella Valley Hiking Club and its members/trail guides.

The trail drops down into a gully and demands that you scramble up the far slope; it's slippery with loose gravel, so caution is advised. Once at the top, favor the faint trail as it climbs to the left and begins taking you above the canyon. As you climb, walk to the west ridge and take in the stunning views of the canyon below. You will continue to follow the trail above the canyon and finally come to a high drop-off looking down into a massive rocky gorge, accented by a plunging waterfall shooting through a narrow rock slot. The trail takes you past the gorge (you can walk down into this gorge and explore to your heart's content, but be careful of the smooth rocks) and, after 0.5 mile, down alongside a tranquil rock-enclosed series of pools—a favored lunch spot—where you can explore farther down canyon in and above the river.

After lunch, climb out to the east and rejoin the trail for a wild hike above a series of rock gorges and waterfalls. Continue to take extra care, as the rock is loose and the sand slippery. After another 0.5 mile, the trail drops almost into the stream. Here you can exit this trail by bushwhacking to the southeast for a distance of less than 100 yards, where you will join the main Palm Canyon Trail, found here as a roadlike pathway.

Take the Palm Canyon Trail north; it eventually follows a wash and connects to where you first crossed this same wash earlier in the day. Look for the rock ducks on the upper slope, indicating the way back. The Indian Canyons close at 5 p.m., so watch the time if you are planning to hike back through the streambed before reaching this main section of the trail for the hike to the trading post.

The tranquil pools at Lost Paradise ensure this as a favored lunch spot

20 *Palm Canyon Trail to Bullseye Rock*

(see map on page 56)

LENGTH: 8 miles	**SEASON:** September to April
HIKING TIME: 5 hours	**INFORMATION:** BLM Office,
ELEVATION GAIN: 700 feet	Palm Springs, (760) 251-4800
DIFFICULTY: Moderate	

For centuries, the Agua Caliente Indians inhabited the magnificent canyon lands south of Palm Springs and Palm Canyon. You may expect to find some artifacts and signs of human habitation somewhere in or near Palm Canyon, and on this hike you do. The main draw, however, continues to be the stunning and expansive scenery, as Palm Canyon is ringed by dozens of adjacent canyons and looks up toward the high-country mountains of Desert Divide and San Jacinto Mountain. The destination of this hike is a large, rounded, granite slab known as Bullseye Rock, which thrusts up from the canyon floor. A stream flows beneath its towering mass and encourages the lush, junglelike growth found in this section of upper Palm Canyon. A fire in 1994 severely burned this area, so vegetation is only now making a comeback.

DIRECTIONS   Follow the directions for Hike 21.

Palm Canyon Gorge

Once on the trail, continue on the southeast canyon fork (the main Palm Canyon Trail) until reaching the sign directing you up the southern hillside and into the backcountry (see Hike 19).

This trail is best done with someone who has been to Bullseye Rock before, as some bushwhacking is required. Follow the Palm Canyon Trail for almost 1.5 miles after climbing out of the main palm-filled canyon. You will eventually come to a steep gully on your right, which is marked with rock ducks. Follow this gully down the 20 to 30 yards to the small stream, then cross over, keeping a close watch for the trail on the other side. This trail takes you up a hill and onto a plateau known as Indian Potrero. It was here in a small village that the Agua Caliente Indians once resided. All that remains are several grinding stones 12 to 16 inches deep, formed in some of the surrounding rocks. The trail climbs higher into the backcountry until reaching a small stream drainage and follows this rivulet to Bullseye Rock, the obvious round granite mass to your left. You can ascend this rock without a rope, but a 75-foot length will assist you around the more difficult challenges. Lunch at the top for a great view of the canyon country around you, or continue exploring on the trail, but note that cactus infestation is thick in these parts and that the trail is sometimes difficult to follow.

21 *Lower Palm Canyon Trail*
(see map on page 56)

LENGTH: 4 miles

HIKING TIME: 4 hours

ELEVATION GAIN: 400 feet

DIFFICULTY: Strenuous

SEASON: September to June

INFORMATION: Indian Canyons Tollgate, Agua Caliente Indians, Palm Springs

This is a wild canyon scramble through twisted rock formations, along and sometimes in a rushing stream, with lush groves of massive Washingtonia palms providing a junglelike setting. Palm Canyon is the jewel of the many canyon hikes found in the sprawling Agua Caliente Indian Canyons south of Palm Springs. It is not as easy a hike as it looks. The rocks are very slippery, and the current can be surprisingly strong during peak snowmelt and runoff. Families can do this hike only by staying above the stream, and only adventurous hikers who are used to negotiating rock obstacles and scrambling through water hazards should continue into the right fork canyon as described here.

DIRECTIONS To reach the trailhead, drive through Palm Springs on Hwy. 111 until reaching the juncture with South Palm Canyon Drive. Turn onto South Palm Canyon Drive and proceed 2 miles to the Indian Canyons tollgate, then continue 2.5 miles to Palm Canyon and the trading post. The trail begins down the walkway from the trading post and to the right.

For the first 0.75 mile you are treated to a pathway above the stream; contorted rock formations which act as the riverbed; assorted pools (and often sunbathers); and a stunning concentration of palm trees, vines, cottonwoods, and desert plants, made possible by the abundant water supply.

Palm Canyon is lined for miles with 2,000-year-old Washingtonia palms

As the trail reaches back into the canyon, you will eventually come to the first major canyon fork on the right. This is where only serious hikers (and mountain goats) should tread. You can follow Lower Palm Canyon for miles, but the first 2 miles should provide challenge enough. There are deep pools to hike through or around, tricky cliff formations to navigate, huge boulders to scramble over, and plenty of swimming holes to try. Caution: Until sometime in March the water is COLD snowmelt. After that, water levels subside, water temperatures rise, and the trip gets a whole lot easier! Be prepared to encounter small groups of gutsy day hikers, college kids, and isolated sun worshipers . . . this canyon is no secret!

Lower Palm Canyon makes the perfect "adventure" hike for those prepared to deal with challenges, and a great picnic getaway for those inclined to spend a warm spring day lazing on the rocks beside shimmering canyon pools.

22 *Murray Canyon Trail*

LENGTH: 6 miles

HIKING TIME: 4 hours

ELEVATION GAIN: 500 feet

DIFFICULTY: Moderate

SEASON: September to June

INFORMATION: Indian Canyons Tollgate, Agua Caliente Indians, Palm Springs

Murray Canyon Trail takes you deep into the lower reaches of the San Jacinto Mountains via a palm-enclosed canyon stream found on the Agua Caliente Indian Reservation in south Palm Springs. This canyon differs somewhat from its close neighbor, Andreas Canyon, by offering the hiker many more miles of trail on which to explore higher canyon elevations. The California fan palm is quite abundant in Murray, giving another lush escape from the surrounding desert heat. This hike requires more caution during high spring runoff, as the streambeds tend to challenge the trail at several crossings. You can also travel farther up Murray Canyon in bushwhacking style, depending on the thickness of the undergrowth, the strength of the rushing waters, and your own adventurous spirit.

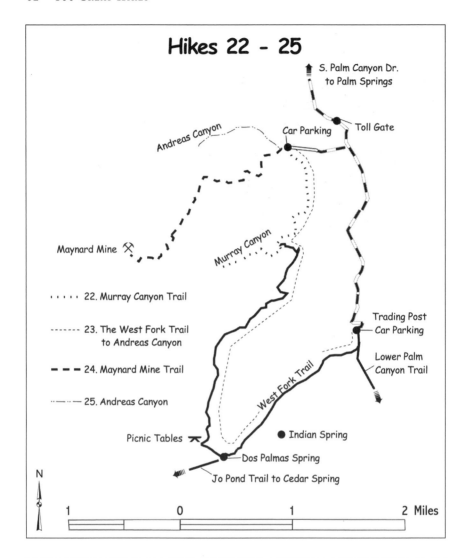

Hikes 22 - 25

S. Palm Canyon Dr.
to Palm Springs

Toll Gate

Car Parking

Andreas Canyon

Maynard Mine

Murray Canyon

· · · · · 22. Murray Canyon Trail

- - - - - - 23. The West Fork Trail
to Andreas Canyon

▬ ▬ ▬ 24. Maynard Mine Trail

·—·—· 25. Andreas Canyon

Trading Post
Car Parking

Lower Palm
Canyon Trail

West Fork Trail

Picnic Tables

● Indian Spring

Dos Palmas Spring

Jo Pond Trail to Cedar Spring

N

1   0   1   2 Miles

DIRECTIONS   Reach this trail by following directions for Andreas Canyon (Hike 25), found at the south end of Palm Springs in the Agua Caliente Indian Canyons, 2 miles south of Hwy. 111 on South Palm Canyon Drive.

When you reach Andreas Canyon, cross the stream and follow the signs south of the river. The trail meanders a while through the underbrush and along the stream before beginning to break away from its sister canyon and head in a more southwest direction. Desert willow, assorted cacti, and a scattering of cottonwood are found along the river. Take extra care along this waterway during

strong and high runoff; hikers have been injured on the slippery rocks and in the deep water. This hike makes a great picnic adventure and treats you to the vistas of high canyon country and soaring cliffs.

Rocky terrain lines this canyon bottom

23 *The West Fork Trail to Andreas Canyon*

LENGTH: 10 miles

HIKING TIME: 6 hours

ELEVATION GAIN: 2,500 feet

DIFFICULTY: Strenuous

SEASON: October to April

INFORMATION: BLM Office, Palm Springs, (760) 251-4800

The West Fork/Jo Pond Trail climbs dramatically and steeply upward out of Palm Canyon, eventually reaching the Pacific Crest Trail and Desert Divide, 6,000 feet above the valley floor. After 2 miles, the trail joins with another section heading north and climbs to reach a maximum elevation gain of 2,500 feet. By taking this right fork the hiker can make his or her way back to Andreas Canyon, thereby requiring a shuttle or car to be parked there and at the Indian Trading Post in Palm Canyon. You are treated to the most magnificent vistas of the high country above Palm Springs, as well as the long, palm-filled canyons below.

DIRECTIONS

To begin, head to the Agua Caliente Indian Canyons south of town described in Hike 21.

Small mountain streams serve as minor obstacles to hikers

Just after several hundred yards down the Palm Canyon Trail, look to the right for a signpost which marks the beginning of the West Fork Trail.

You will climb through a wonderland of rocks and mountain vegetation—note as you ascend how quickly the scenery opens up below you. This trail is steep and strenuous. It can be demanding in warm weather. Hikers should take plenty of water and be careful of overextending themselves on a hot day.

After 2 miles take the trail to the right (northwest). The trail takes you to a lovely picnic table alongside a rushing stream, surrounded by lush greenery. This could be the halfway point for hikers not wishing to do the total 10 miles or who have not made provisions for a shuttle.

From here the trail picks up across the stream and begins another rapid ascent up the mountain. The views will continue to amaze you. During late winter the slopes are ablaze with flowers and by spring the cacti follow suit. You will continue on this trail until it begins to emerge overlooking Murray Canyon to the north. The trail then descends to the lower slopes and crosses several streams, notably Murray Canyon. You might find the crossing difficult in wet winters, but continue downstream until you connect with a good crossing point. The trail picks up on the other side and eventually joins with the Murray Canyon Trail, taking you back to the parking lot in Andreas Canyon.

24 *Maynard Mine Trail*

(see map on page 62)

LENGTH: 10 miles

HIKING TIME: 6 hours

ELEVATION GAIN: 2,200 feet

DIFFICULTY: Strenuous

SEASON: October to April

INFORMATION: BLM Office, Palm Springs, (760) 251-4800

Alongside the mountainous ridge which rises above Murray Canyon on the western side of Agua Caliente Indian Canyons is a rugged trail leading up to the remains of an old tungsten mine, worked during World War II and known as the Maynard Mine after its developer, Jim Maynard. This hike not only takes you to the scattered remains of the mine, but also gives you great views of the canyon slopes across Palm Canyon Valley as well as the snowy ridgeline of Desert Divide. This is a great winter hike, taking you close to the Pacific Crest Trail above the valley, while showing you the swirling clouds and storms associated with the upper ridge.

DIRECTIONS To reach this trail, follow the directions for entering the Agua Caliente Indian Canyons given in Hike 25. Park at the Andreas Canyon parking area, cross the stream at the road walkway, and look for signs to Murray Canyon.

Listed in the National Register of Historic Places, Indian Canyon and its surrounding Palm and Andreas canyons feature the most palm trees of any canyon in the world

Begin on the Murray Canyon Trail as it makes its way quickly up the mountain. In short order you will come to a rock marker indicating a trail rising from the Murray Canyon Trail and heading in a steep fashion up another ridge. This is the Maynard Mine Trail.

The climb up the slope is relentless—nothing gradual about it. No shade covering is offered so hikers doing this trail in October or on a warm March day must be prepared for warm weather hiking. Essentially, you will be hiking on slopes where the heat is reflected back by the rocks. After 5 miles you will reach your objective, the Maynard Mine.

All that remains is a 10-foot-deep hole for you to examine, and an old gas-powered engine, rather large, suggesting the strenuous work it took to haul it up the same slope you just hiked. Return by the same trail, treated to the many beautiful vistas of the valley and the distant peaks to the south.

25 *Andreas Canyon*

(see map on page 62)

LENGTH: 2 miles

HIKING TIME: 2 hours

ELEVATION GAIN: 50 feet

DIFFICULTY: Easy

SEASON: September to June

INFORMATION: Indian Canyons Tollgate, Agua Caliente Indians, Palm Springs

Tucked away in the southwestern corner of Palm Springs is a hiker's paradise, known locally as the Indian Canyons and situated on several thousand acres of the Agua Caliente Indian Reservation. The canyons join with the foothills of the soaring San Jacinto Mountains rising from the canyon floor and culminating in the 10,801-foot San Jacinto Peak. The Pacific Crest Trail looks down into these canyons from Desert Divide, the south by southwest mountain ridge which borders the reservation, and, during the winter, torrents of water wash through the canyons below. Many spectacular hikes begin or end in these canyons. One of the shorter but still quite lovely hikes is the Andreas Canyon hike, found less than a mile from the tollgate. This trail follows a stream (sometimes a river during peak mountain runoff) while winding through hundreds of native California fan palms. The towering snowcapped mountains above suggest to the hiker that countless hiking adventures await at higher elevations.

DIRECTIONS   To reach Andreas Canyon, drive south onto South Palm Canyon Drive where it meets Hwy. 111 in the south end of Palm Springs. Follow the signs to the Agua Caliente Indian Canyons, and after paying the toll, take the road to the right 0.75 mile to the picnic tables.

The trail follows the right side of the stream and crosses over several times before bringing you to a wire fence exactly 1 mile from the start. This stream can be quite high after heavy rainfall or when the snows melt in the mountains above the desert, usually in late February. The lush palms, vines, and bushes along the stream suggest a more tropical setting and contrast sharply with the desert below. Be careful of slippery rocks and hard-to-negotiate places. Andreas makes a great picnic or romantic get-away hike . . . but even the kids will find

high adventure as they make their way under towering cliffs and through the rushing stream. March, early April, and late October are especially fine times to hike this and other trails found in the Indian Canyons.

The Palms entrance of Andreas Canyon

26 *The Hahn–Buena Vista Loop*

LENGTH: 16 miles

HIKING TIME: 8 hours

ELEVATION GAIN: 2,000 feet

DIFFICULTY: Strenuous

SEASON: October to May

INFORMATION: BLM Office, Palm Springs, (760) 251-4800

The Hahn–Buena Vista Loop was named after Jean Hahn, a member of the Desert Riders and an ardent equestrian. Buena Vista translates into "good view," and the 360 degree vistas afforded by this trail validate this choice of names. The trail itself is an isolated segment of the much larger network of trails surrounding the Murray Hill area east of Palm Canyon, and on the westernmost reaches of the Santa Rosa Mountains.

DIRECTIONS   To reach this beautiful section of trail, follow the directions for Hike 18 to where the Wildhorse Trail joins the secondary wash.

Hikers should expect to traverse seasonal waterfalls in this section of the Santa Rosas

From here go left to the signpost for the Vandeventer/Hahn–Buena Vista Loop, turn right, and follow the trail as it meanders through small washes and up short slopes to a "Y" intersection. Go left here, making what appears to be a northwest jaunt to Dunn Road.

At Dunn Road turn right (south) and continue to where the Art Smith Trail joins it. You will find some much appreciated picnic tables where you can rest. Turn right off Dunn Road and begin following the Hahn–Buena Vista Loop back to the Wildhorse Trail and your eventual starting point. The views here are spectacular, and in a wet spring, wildflowers and blooming cacti accent the area.

This section of trail, as well as all the Murray Hill trail network, tends to warm up quite a bit on most fall or spring afternoons, so come prepared with adequate water and food.

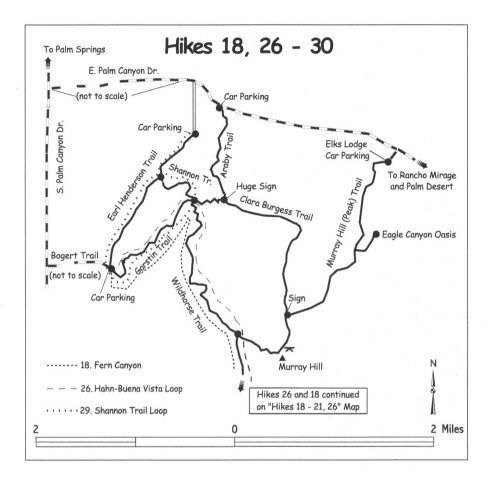

Hikes 18, 26 - 30

To Palm Springs
E. Palm Canyon Dr.
(not to scale)
S. Palm Canyon Dr.
Car Parking
Car Parking
Earl Henderson Trail
Shannon Tr.
Araby Trail
Huge Sign
Clara Burgess Trail
Elks Lodge
Car Parking
To Rancho Mirage
and Palm Desert
Eagle Canyon Oasis
Murray Hill (Peak) Trail
Bogert Trail
(not to scale)
Garstin Trail
Car Parking
Wildhorse Trail
Sign
Murray Hill

- - - - - - - 18. Fern Canyon
— — — 26. Hahn-Buena Vista Loop
· · · · · · 29. Shannon Trail Loop

N

Hikes 26 and 18 continued
on "Hikes 18 - 21, 26" Map

2   0   2 Miles

27 *Murray Hill (Peak)*

LENGTH: 10 miles

HIKING TIME: 5 hours

ELEVATION GAIN: 2,100 feet

DIFFICULTY: Strenuous

SEASON: October to April

INFORMATION: BLM Office,
Palm Springs, (760) 251-4800

It's difficult to call Murray Hill anything but a "peak," yet officially it's a hill on all the maps. Unofficially, after climbing the 2,100 feet to the top, you'll think of it more like a PEAK! The views are magnificent, showing the region around Palm Springs, Cathedral City, and Palm Canyon, while offering you the nearby San Jacinto Mountains to the west.

DIRECTIONS

To reach the trail, drive on Hwy. 111 in the east section of Palm Springs and turn south on Elk Trail. Park behind the 1905 Elks Lodge and hike up 200 feet in the steep, rocky canyon, staying to the left side of the canyon.

At the top there is a pile of concrete pieces; head left toward the wrecked yellow bulldozer. Follow the trail up the old road to the trailhead at the top. Continue along the old jeep road in an easterly direction, making a partial circle around a small hill. Look southeast to see the looming singular massif of Murray Hill. Very shortly up the road to the left is a rock cairn. Follow the trail down into Eagle Canyon. In spring this area can be a sea of yellow from the abundant brittlebush and other desert flowers. Continue to a "Y" intersection. To the left is the Eagle Canyon palm oasis; continue following the Eagle Canyon Trail up and to the right 0.5 mile until you reach the Eagle Canyon/Palm Canyon/McManis trail signs. Follow the trail down to the wash at the bottom of Eagle Canyon and out the other side (north, or left). The trail follows a bit of ridge until you see the Clara Burgess trailhead sign. Take this trail up the remaining 2 miles to the top of Murray Hill.

Picnic tables await you at the top, as does a stunning 360 degree view of the surrounding deserts, Dunn Road to the south, and the stately San Jacinto Mountains due west. To return, you can retrace your route or continue south on the Clara Burgess Trail, down the south side of Murray Hill to the trail sign. From here, hike in a westerly direction along a beautiful ridge with stunning vistas. At the bottom of the switchbacks, turn right at the huge trail sign, walking in a northerly direction until rejoining Eagle Canyon Trail. From here, you can return the way you came.

A hiker enjoys the view of Murray Hill from West Fork Trail

28 *Earl Henderson Trail*

(see map on page 69)

LENGTH: 4 miles

HIKING TIME: 3 hours

ELEVATION GAIN: 400 feet

DIFFICULTY: Easy

SEASON: October to May

INFORMATION: BLM Office, Palm Springs, (760) 251-4800

This trail is one of the many interconnecting trails found on the ridges and plateaus surrounding Murray Hill, east of Palm Canyon. The trail is named after Earl Henderson, past president of the equestrian group the Desert Riders. At the top of this trail, you are rewarded with scenic views of Canyon Country Club, South Palm Springs, and the San Jacinto Mountains thrusting up from the west side of Palm Canyon.

DIRECTIONS

From Palm Desert, go west to Palm Springs via Hwy. 111 and Palm Canyon. Turn left (south) onto Araby Drive, proceed through Palm Canyon Wash, and park on the left-hand side of the road.

Head west up the wash for about 0.25 mile to the Palm Springs Trail sign. Turn left and follow the trail up to the Henderson and Shannon Trail signs. Continue southwest on the Earl Henderson Trail. After 2 miles, the trail ends at the Garstin Trail sign. From here, you are treated to a vista of Palm Springs, Palm Canyon, and Canyon Country Club. This makes a great early morning or evening hike—short, but with just enough elevation gain and good views to make the effort worthwhile.

Hikers sometimes encounter cattle along the trail above Palm Canyon

29 *Shannon Trail Loop*

(see map on page 69)

LENGTH: 7 miles

HIKING TIME: 4 hours

ELEVATION GAIN: 1,000 feet

DIFFICULTY: Moderate

SEASON: October to May

INFORMATION: BLM Office, Palm Springs, (760) 251-4800

Prickly pear cactus in bloom

The Shannon Trail Loop is one of several beautiful variations of hiking loops offered by the unique interconnections of crisscrossing trails found in and around Murray Hill, on the eastern side of Palm Canyon. This loop gives you good views of the Palm Springs area and the nearby San Jacinto Mountains. The trail was named after Shannon Corliss, daughter of the equestrian Desert Riders' past president, Ray Corliss.

DIRECTIONS

To reach the trailhead, drive east on Hwy. 111 toward Palm Springs and turn south (left) onto Araby Drive. Proceed through Palm Canyon Wash and park on the left or south side of the wash.

Head west up the wash for 0.25 mile to the trailhead sign, Palm Springs Trail. Turn left and hike up the switchbacks until reaching the signs for the Earl Henderson and Shannon Trails. From here, view Canyon Country Club and Palm Springs.

To make the loop, continue along the Earl Henderson Trail until reaching the signpost for the Garstin Trail. Follow the Garstin Trail up to the overlooks of South Palm Canyon and the signpost for Wildhorse/Berns/Shannon/Garstin and Palm Canyon. Continue straight ahead in a northerly direction for a short distance to the next signpost, Garstin/Shannon/Henderson. From here, proceed left down the trail, quite steep in places, and take the Shannon/Henderson Trail back down to your starting point. This trail loop makes a wonderful early morning hike in spring, but take care to avoid hot desert afternoons, and always take a good supply of water.

30 *The Araby Trail*
(see map on page 69)

LENGTH: 6 miles

HIKING TIME: 3 hours

ELEVATION GAIN: 800 feet

DIFFICULTY: Moderate

SEASON: October to May

INFORMATION: BLM Office, Palm Springs, (760) 251-4800

Desert vegetation in winter bloom

The Araby Trail could also be dubbed the "trail to the stars," as it climbs above the Bob Hope Estate and the home of the late Steve McQueen. The view of these magnificent homes is readily available on this trail, along with that of Palm Springs. The Araby Trail is another great short but sweet "exercise" trail, allowing you to make the up-and-back trip in under 6 miles.

DIRECTIONS

From Palm Desert, drive west to Palm Springs on Hwy. 111. Turn left (south) at the Rimcrest/Southridge Road and development. The trail can be found on the left (east) side of the road, shortly after turning.

As you hike up the Araby Trail, you are in for 3 miles of spectacular scenery and homes. The trail skirts the home of Bob Hope as it makes its way to the top of the ridge, before connecting with Berns/Garstin/Henderson Trail. At the signpost for these trails, one can return to the trailhead or continue and eventually interconnect with the many other trails found in these foothills. Take plenty of cool water if you do this hike in late spring or early fall—afternoon temperatures can approach 100 degrees.

31 *North and South Lykken Trail*

LENGTH: 9 miles

HIKING TIME: 5 hours

ELEVATION GAIN: 800 feet

DIFFICULTY: Moderate

SEASON: October to March

INFORMATION: BLM Office, Palm Springs, (760) 251-4800

In 1972 the Skyline Trail was renamed the Lykken Trail in honor of Carl Lykken, a Palm Springs pioneer and the town's first postmaster. This magnificent desert view trail travels along the San Jacinto Mountains above Palm Springs, roughly following Palm Canyon Drive. The views of Palm Springs and the valley, which stretch toward the eastern horizon, will be awesome as you negotiate through the rocky terrain, accented in the spring with yellow blooming brittlebush and flowering cacti. En route to the end of the South Lykken Trail, you are treated to fabulous views of Palm Springs and of Tahquitz Canyon, held sacred by the Cahuilla Indians and abounding in vegetation and waterfalls but currently restricted in use because of environmental abuse.

To begin hiking the South Lykken Trail, drive into Palm Springs via Hwy. 111, which becomes Palm Canyon Drive, and turn south onto South Palm Canyon Drive. Proceed south to Canyon Heights Road; 250 feet farther along on the west side of the road is a trail sign. As this is a shuttle hike, cars need to be parked here. The shuttle spot for the Lykken Trail is Cielo Drive off Panorama Road in Palm Springs.

Head west up the trail; before the switchbacks begin, you will come to the trailhead sign. The trail continues for 3 miles before it goes down to street level at Tahquitz Creek. Go north through Tahquitz Creek, following the trail signs (if there has been heavy rainfall or snowmelt, go over the creek by using the cement water dike). Meander over and down La Mirada Street until it meets Ramon Road. This marks the beginning of the North Lykken Trail.

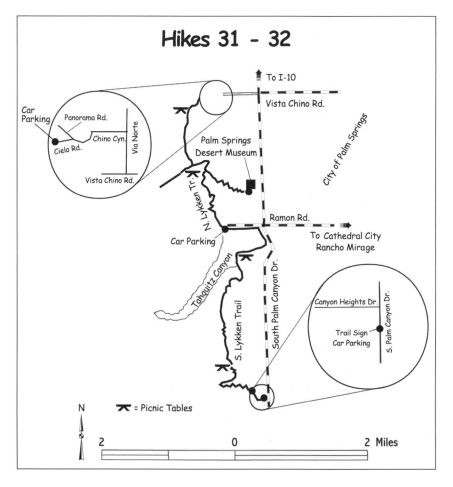

Hikes 31 - 32

To I-10

Vista Chino Rd.

Car Parking

Panorama Rd.

Chino Cyn.

Cielo Rd.

Via Norte

Vista Chino Rd.

Palm Springs Desert Museum

City of Palm Springs

N. Lykken Tr.

Ramon Rd.

Car Parking

To Cathedral City Rancho Mirage

Tahquitz Canyon

S. Lykken Trail

South Palm Canyon Dr.

Canyon Heights Dr.

Trail Sign Car Parking

S. Palm Canyon Dr.

N

⚔ = Picnic Tables

2   0   2 Miles

Yucca in bloom

The trail becomes a switchback as it heads northwesterly toward Chino Canyon. After several miles you will reach the picnic tables overlooking the Palm Springs Desert Museum. Continue to take the trail north, as if heading around the corner of the mountain. The trail meanders down through a wash full of large rock and desert growth. On the other side of the wash you will have a gradual climb toward Chino Canyon, where the trail ends in a subdivision by descending the faint trail on the north side of the picnic table.

There is no shade on this trail so take plenty of cool water.

32 The Palm Springs Desert Museum Trail (see map on page 75)

LENGTH: 2 miles

HIKING TIME: 2 hours

ELEVATION GAIN: 1,000 feet

DIFFICULTY: Moderate

SEASON: October to May

INFORMATION: Palm Springs Desert Museum, (760) 325-0189

DIRECTIONS

To reach the trailhead, drive into Palm Springs on Hwy. 111 until reaching the downtown area. Turn west on Tahquitz Way, then right on Museum Drive. The museum is found directly in back of the Desert Fashion Plaza Mall. The trail begins in the north parking lot of the museum.

The Palm Springs Desert Museum is a cultural landmark in Palm Springs for all valley residents and visitors . . . an oasis of both natural history and desert flora and fauna, offering the finest in art and cultural entertainment. So what better way to immediately involve yourself in the desert hiking scene than by walking out of the Desert Museum and onto the challenging Museum Trail found just outside its front door? The view from the top gives you a great look into the sprawling city of Palm Springs and the desert beyond. Although it's a steep hike of over 1,000 feet in just a mile, if the pace is kept slow and steady, most hikers can reach the picnic tables found at the trail's end with little trouble.

After steeply ascending the mountain, the trail connects with the Carl Lykken Trail.

Hedgehog cactus is commonly found in the desert regions of Southern California

San Jacinto Mountains
Hikes 33 – 61

Trailhead Locations in the
San Jacinto Mountains (Hikes 33 - 61)

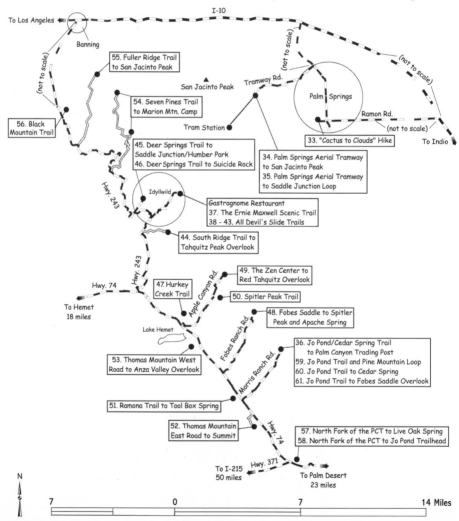

33 *"Cactus to Clouds" Hike*

LENGTH: 22 miles

HIKING TIME: 13 hours

ELEVATION GAIN: 10,400 feet

DIFFICULTY: Very strenuous

SEASON: May to October

INFORMATION: BLM Office, Palm Springs, (760) 251-4800

You crossed the Sahara Desert lately? Swam the Amazon River recently? Ran the Boston Marathon last week? Have we got a challenge for you! In all of the continental United States there is perhaps no higher elevation gain in one day than the "Cactus to Clouds" hike. From the beginning of the trailhead, this hike takes you up, and up, and up, 10,400 feet to the top of San Jacinto Peak . . . all in one day, all 22 miles of it!

The views of the Coachella Valley and surrounding mountain ranges are spectacular. The views of the seemingly impossible top are, too! But be in the best shape of your life to handle this one. One consolation: You get to ride the tram down to Palm Springs, instead of descending those 10,400 feet!

DIRECTIONS

Drive into Palm Springs on Ramon Road from I-10 and park at the road's end. Park a second car at the Palm Springs Aerial Tramway.

Take the Lykken Trail up the switchbacks for about 1.5 miles until you reach a coffee-table size boulder on the left side of the trail. Painted on this boulder is a sign, "Long Valley 8 miles" (Long Valley is the valley adjacent to the Mountain Tram Station at 8,600 elevation).

This section of the trail looks down into Tachevan Canyon to the right (north) for about 2.5 miles. Although this early section of the trail is somewhat easy to find, the remainder of the trail to the top of Long Valley is faint and poorly marked and should be done only with someone who has previously hiked this section. This entire trail is virtually an unending succession of upward-reaching switchbacks—perhaps a respectable "hiking cousin" to the famed 97 switchbacks to Mt. Whitney.

There is no water available on this trail until you reach Long Valley. Up to the ranger station in Long Valley is almost 11 miles (about 8 hours hard hiking). From this point exhausted hikers may opt to make the short walk to the tram station and catch the next tram down to Palm Springs. (Don't feel too bad; many who have attempted the "Cactus to Clouds" saga have done just that.)

If you decide to continue, you will need a wilderness permit from the ranger station. The trail from here is clearly marked and well used. From the ranger station, proceed to Round Valley, then up to Wellman Divide. Here, the last section of the trail takes you almost directly to San Jacinto Peak. One-third mile from the peak is the side trail that will take you to your final destination. Several hundred yards from the peak is a stone cabin that serves as necessary shelter in poor weather conditions.

Once on the peak, you will enjoy a 360 degree view—of what seems like the whole world.

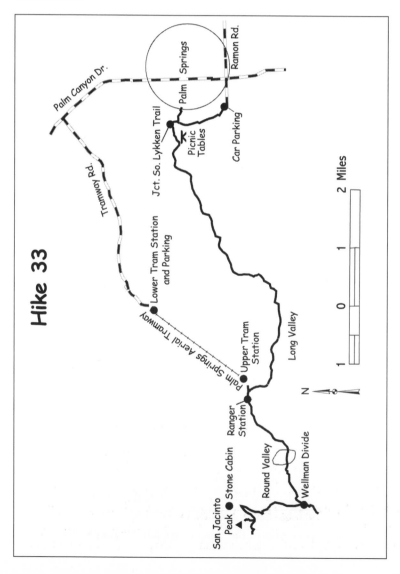

34 *Palm Springs Aerial Tramway to San Jacinto Peak*

LENGTH: 11 miles

HIKING TIME: 6 hours

ELEVATION GAIN: 2,300 feet

DIFFICULTY: Strenuous

SEASON: May to November

INFORMATION: USDA Forest Service, Idyllwild, (909) 659-2117

Famous naturalist John Muir, after climbing to the top of San Jacinto Peak, exclaimed that the view was one of the most sublime spectacles seen anywhere on earth. This kind of endorsement is enough to get any serious hiker up the slope to the top! The peaks in the San Jacinto Mountains are huge granite massifs that remind the well-traveled hiker of the High Sierras, especially the chain of peaks from Lone Pine to Bishop. The 360 degree view from the top gives you a complete reference for all of southern California's mountain and desert landmarks, and on a very clear day you can actually peer into Nevada! The San Jacinto Mountains are relatively young, geologically speaking— perhaps 20 million years young. But the rocks in these mountains have been upthrust from deep within the earth and are perhaps 500 million years old! The hike to the top is varied, with the lower elevations offering sylvan meadows and streams before bringing you to the more demanding final climb up the alpine slopes near the peak.

DIRECTIONS

To begin this adventure, take the Hwy. 111 exit from I-10 into Palm Springs, or take Hwy. 111 from Palm Desert to Palm Springs. From the interstate exit, drive 9 miles to Tramway Road, then turn right and drive until you reach the parking area. Shuttle trams will take you to the tram station on crowded days. After paying the fee, ride the tram to the top, exit at the mountain station, and head toward the ranger station located 0.25 mile to the west. Obtain your day hiking permit, sign in, and take the trail leading to Round Valley.

During the early summer you will cross many streams or travel alongside them, but by early fall most have dried up. The trail winds up through the pine thickets until coming to beautiful Round Valley. Here the grass is deep green, tall, and richly watered—look for deer munching tender plants.

Continue toward the peak by taking the trail to Wellman Divide. This is a short, steep climb that gives you teases of views to come as you look back to the north and east into the desert below. At Wellman Divide the views are spectacular, both of the Tahquitz Peak area and the farther Santa Rosa Mountains.

From this point you are only 2.7 miles from the peak. Follow the trail to the top, up steep switchbacks. The views will continue to amaze, as vistas grow ever more expansive and breathtaking. Near the top there is another trail junction: Take the one for San Jacinto Peak. In a short time you will come to and then pass a stone shelter for those caught in stormy weather. Just up from there is the peak.

Geographers claim that the angle of descent—the steepness of San Jacinto Mountain from top to base—is the sheerest in the United States. From the top looking down, most tend to agree. It can be quite cool at the top, even cold and very windy. Take a windbreaker, a pair of binoculars . . . and enjoy the view!

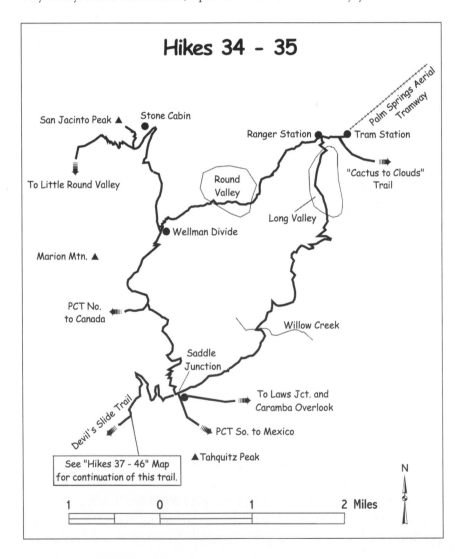

35 *Palm Springs Aerial Tramway to Saddle Junction Loop*

LENGTH: 12 miles

HIKING TIME: 7 hours

ELEVATION GAIN: 3,000 feet

DIFFICULTY: Strenuous

SEASON: May to November

INFORMATION: USDA Forest Service, Idyllwild, (909) 659-2117

The top of San Jacinto Mountain and Wilderness Area is shaped in the form of a bowl, with the western side considerably higher than the eastern. This geographical feature allows hikers to do a magnificent loop hike from the Mountain Tram Station toward Saddle Junction above Idyllwild. The route follows a gradual descent from the high point of the "bowl" at Wellman Divide down to the bottom at Saddle Junction, along the bottom of the valley floor, and then finally up to the northern top ridges near the starting point. Hikers are treated to wide vistas that reinforce the notion of San Jacinto Mountain as being an "island in the sky."

DIRECTIONS

To reach the trailhead, follow directions for Hike 34. Take Hwy. 111 into Palm Springs, turn up Tramway Road, and park. After riding up to the top of the mountain, head for the ranger station 0.25 mile west of the mountain station. Sign in and pick up your wilderness permit for your day hike to Saddle Junction.

Follow the trail up to Wellman Divide. This first 3-mile leg takes you up 1,200 feet through pine forests, along mountain streams that are quite full in early summer, and alongside the lush green grasslands of Round Valley. At Wellman Divide you first glimpse the expansive horizon vistas that will fill your vision for the better part of the next 2.5 miles. The towering granite massif of Tahquitz Peak dominates your view to the southeast.

As you head down the trail you will pass a series of small but delightful springs that flow from the mountainside and encourage a proliferation of ferns, flowers, and grasses. Descending farther, you will pass the junction with the Pacific Crest Trail, then head rapidly down to the pine groves surrounding Saddle Junction. You will usually find a number of hikers gathered here, as this is the main crossroads for the hikes above Idyllwild.

Continue back to the tram by taking the trail from Saddle Junction north and west of Skunk Cabbage Meadows. This section of trail is populated by huge ponderosa pines, some say the largest in California. You will soon come to the cool waters of Willow Creek. Take a good rest here; for the next 2 miles the trail winds steadily up the mountain, but offers you good views of the Desert Divide and Santa Rosa Mountains to the southeast. You will finally reach the top of the "bowl" and can soon see the tram station in the near distance. Take at least 3 quarts of water, since this hike begins cool but ends warm.

East face of the majestic San Jacinto Mountain

36 Jo Pond/Cedar Spring Trail to Palm Canyon Trading Post

LENGTH: 13 miles

HIKING TIME: 8 hours

ELEVATION GAIN: 1,300 feet

ELEVATION LOSS: 5,850 feet

DIFFICULTY: Strenuous

SEASON: October to April

INFORMATION: BLM Office, Palm Springs, (760) 251-4800

DIRECTIONS

To reach the trailhead, drive 28 miles south on Hwy. 74 from Palm Desert and Hwy. 111, or almost 11 miles east of Mountain Center on Hwy. 74 if you come from Hemet. Turn north onto Morris Ranch Road at the CDF Fire Station, and proceed 3 miles to the sign that reads "Park Off Pavement." After parking, pick up the trail for Cedar Spring just a few hundred yards up the road.

For sheer, majestic vistas and spectacular spring flora, few trails in or near the Coachella Valley match the Jo Pond/Cedar Spring Trail, with its entire length stretching from atop the Desert Divide Ridge/Pacific Crest Trail (PCT) to the Indian Trading Post in Palm Canyon. This is a shuttle hike. Someone must drop you off at the Cedar Spring Trailhead in Garner Valley and pick you up at the Indian Trading Post in Palm Canyon.

The best time for this adventurous hike, in regard to temperature, flora, and river runoff, is March to mid-April. The views are inspiring and beautiful as you hike up and over the Desert Divide Ridge, make your way along West Fork Canyon, and finally emerge over the sprawl of Palm Canyon before reaching the trading post at the canyon's head. Take your camera, hope that the snow is still blanketing the higher peaks, and be prepared for the rigors of an almost 6,000-foot drop in elevation— protect those knees and toes!

The trees of Cedar Spring Grove provide a shady resting spot for fatigued hikers

You spend the first 0.5 mile walking through beautiful oak woods, along a rushing stream and over a stunning meadow before beginning the ascent up the slope to the PCT and Desert Divide Ridge. At the trail's beginning, a large sign marking the southern terminus of the newly built Jo Pond Trail indicates 3 miles to Cedar Spring, 7 to the picnic tables above West Fork Canyon, and 12.5 to the Indian Trading Post (it says 15 miles to the tollgate, which is 2.5 miles beyond the trading post).

As you climb toward the PCT, looking south you can see the Palomar Mountain Observatory atop Palomar Mountain and sections of Garner Valley. Once you're at the crest, and as you begin your descent over the ridge, the entire Coachella Valley spreads out before you, with Palm Canyon's 16-mile length snaking its way far below to the east. After a mile you will reach the cool incense cedar grove and camping area of Cedar Spring. From here the trail should be signed, indicating a climb from the campground, along a stream/gully, and eventually over to the burned mountainous area northwest of Cedar Spring, consumed by the July 1994 fire.

Once over this section, you will be hiking along the Garnet Ridge for 3 to 4 miles, with awesome high-country views of the entire length of the San Jacinto Mountains to the west, made especially scenic by a thick winter snow cover. Palm Canyon will continue to amaze you as you look east, with noticeable green patches, tree-filled canyons, and the obvious meandering trail along its bottom.

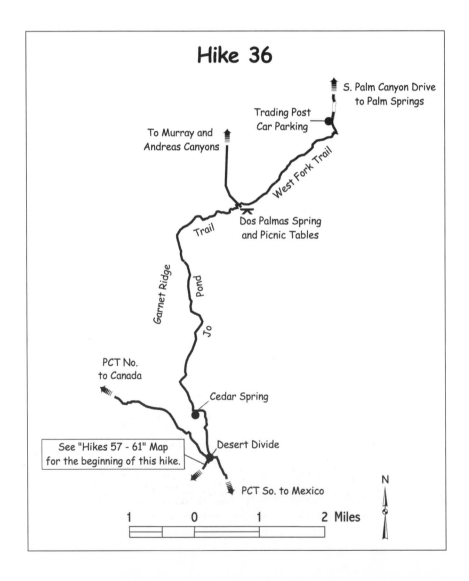

After the trail steeply drops for 7 miles down the ridge, with dozens of switchbacks, you will reach a beautiful picnic area and overlook, complete with several picnic tables . . . a great, natural lunch stop. From here the scenery really captures your aesthetic senses, as the trail comes down along the West Fork Canyon and offers you green valleys, waterfalls, grass-covered slopes, oases, stunning verdant canyons, flowers, and flowering cacti. This part of the hike is more like a trip through a nature preserve than through "desert canyons"!

After almost 12 miles, you'll finally come over the ridge and look into verdant Palm Canyon. The trail quickly takes you to the canyon's bottom along a short section of raging stream and up to the Indian Trading Post for a richly deserved cool drink. This hike does test your ability to come down a steep trail . . . strong knees are a must!

37 *The Ernie Maxwell Scenic Trail*

LENGTH: 5 miles

HIKING TIME: 3 hours

ELEVATION GAIN: 300 feet

DIFFICULTY: Easy

SEASON: May to November

INFORMATION: USDA Forest Service, Idyllwild, (909) 659-2117

A popular rock-climbing spot, Suicide Rock offers over 200 different climbing routes

The Ernie Maxwell Scenic Trail is the perfect leisurely hike, especially for families. This trail is marked by gentle contours, an occasional stream, and a generous mix of Jeffrey, ponderosa, and Coulter pines, with some incense cedar and fir. The trail bears the name of a local Idyllwild resident, Ernie Maxwell, to honor his pioneering conservation efforts and his love of the surrounding mountains.

DIRECTIONS

To hike this trail, follow the directions for Hike 39, taking Fern Valley Road out of Idyllwild. Just before reaching the topmost parking area, you will see the sign marking the entrance to the Ernie Maxwell Trail. No permit is needed for this trail.

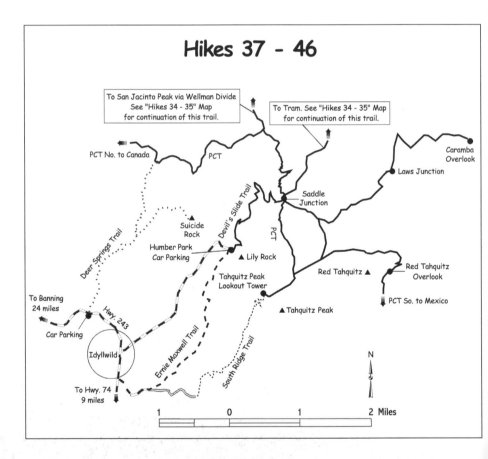

Hikes 37 - 46

To San Jacinto Peak via Wellman Divide
See "Hikes 34 - 35" Map
for continuation of this trail.

To Tram. See "Hikes 34 - 35" Map
for continuation of this trail.

PCT No. to Canada

PCT

Caramba Overlook

Laws Junction

Saddle Junction

Deer Springs Trail

Devil's Slide Trail

Suicide Rock

Humber Park Car Parking

Lily Rock

PCT

Tahquitz Peak Lookout Tower

Red Tahquitz

Red Tahquitz Overlook

To Banning 24 miles

Car Parking

Hwy. 243

Tahquitz Peak

PCT So. to Mexico

Idyllwild

Ernie Maxwell Trail

South Ridge Trail

N

To Hwy. 74 9 miles

1   0   1   2 Miles

Enjoy the gentle, quiet trail as it works its way through the forest thickets; September and October are especially nice months for walking this scenic route. The trail ends at a dirt road, where you simply return to the trailhead.

38 *Humber Park – Devil's Slide Trail to Caramba Overlook*

LENGTH: 14 miles

HIKING TIME: 8 hours

ELEVATION GAIN: 3,400 feet

DIFFICULTY: Strenuous

SEASON: June to November

INFORMATION: USDA Forest Service, Idyllwild, (909) 659-2117

San Jacinto Mountain stands like a cool sentinel rising from the hot desert floor of Coachella Valley. From late spring to early fall, hikers refresh themselves in the forests 8,000 feet above the valley floor, and after hiking to one of the most spectacular desert overlooks at Caramba, they gaze with relief into the searing deserts below. The view stretches eastward all the way to the Salton Sea, while encompassing the Santa Rosa Mountains to the south.

DIRECTIONS
To make this spectacular hike to the overlook, follow the trail directions for Hike 39. This hike requires a wilderness permit, which can be picked up at the ranger station in downtown Idyllwild.

The desert floor spreads out below Idyllwild

After 2.5 miles you will come to the Saddle Junction intersection. Head for Laws Junction through and past the lovely Tahquitz Creek Valley, with its running streams and lush emerald grasses. After 4.7 miles you will reach Laws Junction, which makes a perfect lunch spot, highlighted by the beautiful sylvan water setting of Willow Creek.

The trail to Caramba Overlook leaves from Laws Junction and is a 2-mile descent through thinning forests to the rock formations known as Caramba. If the winter has been wet, you can find good water in nearby Tahquitz Creek, and even a running waterfall found by scrambling down from Caramba. This can be a very hot trail at the height of summer, so come prepared with an ample supply of water.

From Caramba, view the quiet desert below and the distant mountain ranges surrounding the Coachella Valley before starting the long climb back to Idyllwild.

39 *Devil's Slide Trail to Saddle Junction*
(see map on page 88)

LENGTH: 5 miles	**SEASON:** May to November
HIKING TIME: 3 hours	**INFORMATION:** USDA Forest Service, Idyllwild, (909) 659-2117
ELEVATION GAIN: 1,700 feet	
DIFFICULTY: Moderate	

Suicide Rock as viewed from Devil's Slide Trail

Devil's Slide Trail is the most frequently used access trail to the glorious hiking and sylvan beauty found in the San Jacinto Wilderness area and along the many miles of trail which crisscross San Jacinto Mountain. From this trail, the hiker gets wonderful views of Marion Mountain and Suicide and Lily rocks, as well as great exercise in the short distance of 2.5 miles. By reaching Saddle Junction you will be at the main focal point of several key trails heading off in all directions, including the Pacific Crest Trail. Because this trail is very well used, especially during summer, day permits for the Devil's Slide Trail are limited on weekends and holidays between Memorial Day and Labor Day and need to be picked up at the Forest Service Office in Idyllwild.

DIRECTIONS

To reach this trailhead, drive into Idyllwild from Hwy. 243 from Banning and I-10, or take Hwy. 74 and 243 from Palm Desert. In Idyllwild, turn east on North Circle Drive (at The Fort Retail Shopping Center). Proceed north for over a mile until you reach South Circle Drive. Turn right, and then take your first left onto Fern Valley Road. Take the Fern Valley Road to Humber Park (about 2 miles from downtown). Park as the road begins to turn around at the trailhead and loop back on itself. Be advised that on busy weekends you need to get there early.

The trail starts right up the mountain along a series of steep switchbacks. You can see Suicide Rock to your left and the huge granite monolith of Lily Rock to your right rear . . . both popular for serious rock climbers.

The trail crosses six or seven small streams flowing down the mountainside, some of which will flow all summer if the snowfall was heavy. The views are breathtaking as you look back down into Idyllwild and to the south. It may be only 2.5 miles to the top, but if you explore around Saddle Junction in the morning and descend late afternoon during the summer, it can be quite hot, so carry a good supply of water.

For years, Devil's Slide and the generous trail system found at the top have offered a cool respite for the desert dwellers of nearby Coachella Valley. The perfect ending to the perfect day is a well-deserved late lunch at one of the many fine restaurants in Idyllwild.

40 *Devil's Slide Trail to Tahquitz Peak Lookout Loop* (see map on page 88)

LENGTH: 13 miles

HIKING TIME: 7 hours

ELEVATION GAIN: 2,500 feet

DIFFICULTY: Strenuous

SEASON: May to November

INFORMATION: USDA Forest Service, Idyllwild, (909) 659-2117

This loop hike gives the hiker a chance to see the full range of peaks and valley views from the southern portion of San Jacinto Mountain and Wilderness Area. It is a strenuous full day of exploring the ridges and vistas found above Idyllwild and can be either a shuttle from the Devil's Slide Trailhead to Tahquitz Peak Lookout and down to South Ridge Road, where cars can be parked at both trailheads, or a full loop made by returning to Humber Park via the Ernie Maxwell Scenic Trail.

DIRECTIONS   To begin this demanding yet spectacular loop, follow the directions for Hike 39. This hike requires a permit from the Forest Service Office in Idyllwild and a maximum of 15 is allowed in any one party.

After reaching Saddle Junction, take the trail to the right for Tahquitz Peak. During the next mile-plus, you will gradually ascend along a ridge that affords you dramatic views of the desert to the north and the flanking eastern slopes of San Jacinto Mountain. You reach a crossroads of several trails after hiking 1.4 miles.

This loop hike offers views of a full range of peaks and valleys, including South Ridge and Lily Rock

From there take the trail to the south as it makes its way up to the Tahquitz Peak Lookout. This section of the hike is dominated by granite mountains and steep slopes, less forested than at lower elevations. After reaching the lookout tower, head down the trail to South Ridge Trailhead. If you made this a full loop and not a shuttle, then once down South Ridge Road to where it meets Tahquitz View Drive, turn right up the road for about a mile until it meets the south end of the Ernie Maxwell Trail. This is the trail that will take you back to your vehicle at Humber Park.

41 *Devil's Slide Trail to Laws Junction*

(see map on page 88)

LENGTH: 10 miles

HIKING TIME: 5 hours

ELEVATION GAIN: 2,000 feet

DIFFICULTY: Strenuous

SEASON: May to November

INFORMATION: USDA Forest Service, Idyllwild, (909) 659-2117

The lush green meadows and scented pine forests of Tahquitz Valley invite the hiker to escape the warm summer lowlands of Southern California and the blistering desert of the Coachella Valley. Once at the top, you are treated to soft green and celery-colored grasses and a scattering of ferns and skunk cabbage, all watered by the cool mountain streams of Tahquitz and Willow Creek.

DIRECTIONS To reach this sylvan paradise, follow the directions for Hike 39.

Take the Devil's Slide Trail to Saddle Junction. There, the trail divides into several routes. Take the middle route to Laws Junction. In about a mile you will reach the cool, green meadows of Tahquitz Valley and Tahquitz Creek. As you head north toward Laws Junction, you will see a grassy field to your right surrounding a small rocky outcropping. Make for the rocks and enjoy a quiet snack next to Tahquitz Creek; deer often are seen drinking at the water's edge.

Continue down the trail through great stands of ponderosa pine until you reach Laws Junction. Lunch alongside beautiful Willow Creek. This is a spot of rare beauty—cool, serene, and a welcome halfway spot during a warm summer's day.

The route back is best made by following the trail left, avoiding the trail to Caramba Overlook. After a peaceful lunch you might find this section tiring, as it rapidly and unrelentingly climbs from the valley floor back to the trail heading south to Saddle Junction. You are rewarded, however, by several stream cross-

ings and a picturesque look into the desert below. Be sure to take adequate cool water, since these mountain trails can be very hot in summer. A day permit is required for this and every hike that begins with the Devil's Slide Trail.

The lush green meadows near Saddle Junction entice hikers away from the blistering heat of the desert

42 Devil's Slide Trail to Red Tahquitz Overlook *(see map on page 88)*

LENGTH: 11 miles

HIKING TIME: 6 hours

ELEVATION GAIN: 2,000 feet

DIFFICULTY: Strenuous

SEASON: May to November

INFORMATION: USDA Forest Service, Idyllwild, (909) 659-2117

This series of trails leads to an overlook near Red Tahquitz Mountain and gives the hiker great views of the Desert Divide Ridge, the Santa Rosa Mountains, and Tahquitz Valley. The trail takes you into the backcountry, onto the Pacific Crest Trail (PCT), and finally down through the cool, green watershed of Tahquitz Valley and Tahquitz Creek. This day hike allows you to feel and experience the wide diversity of all the various mountain ecosystems found along the southern and eastern flanks of the San Jacinto Mountain Wilderness.

DIRECTIONS

Begin this wonderful hike by following the directions for Hike 39.

Make your way up to Saddle Junction, and take the far right trail toward Tahquitz Peak for 1.4 miles until you reach the junction. Head down and east toward the trail for Red Tahquitz and Little Tahquitz Valley. The views here are wide and magnificent as you head into the valley. At the first junction turn right, up along the PCT. After one mile you will come to a large fallen dead tree along the right side of the trail. Look up and to your right, and begin bushwhacking up the 50 feet of slope, down a small gully, and up again until the high ground is reached. This is the lookout over the entire Desert Ridge Trail. You don't actually reach Red Tahquitz Peak, but this lunch spot offers stunning views to reward your scramble.

When returning, follow the trail down into Tahquitz Valley, then go left where the sign indicates a return back to Saddle Junction. The lush green here offers a stark contrast to the rocky overlook near Red Tahquitz Peak.

Marion Peak, viewed here from the Pacific Crest Trail, towers at over 10,000 feet

43 *Devil's Slide Trail to San Jacinto Peak*

(see map on page 88)

LENGTH: 16 miles

HIKING TIME: 7 – 8 hours

ELEVATION GAIN: 4,400 feet

DIFFICULTY: Strenuous "Adventure Hike"

SEASON: June to October

INFORMATION: USDA Forest Service, Idyllwild, (909) 659-2117

DIRECTIONS Follow the directions for Hike 39.

After parking at Humber Park, begin this adventure hike by taking the Devil's Slide Trail 1,700 feet and 2.5 miles up to Saddle Junction. From there, turn left toward San Jacinto Peak, making your way through white fir and Jeffrey pine, with spectacular views of Lily Rock and Tahquitz Peak. In 2 miles you will reach the trail going left to Strawberry Cienaga, but continue past this side trail toward Wellman Divide.

As you approach the divide, droplets of water often flow from above, over the thick moss to the left of the trail. At Wellman Divide the trail continues up and left toward San Jacinto Peak while another right branch drops down toward Round Valley and the tram station. On the way up the trail you will continue to get great views of the surrounding peaks and the San Jacinto Mountain high country, until coming to the last section of trail, a short "peak" trail that passes a stone cabin, which is 0.2 mile to the peak.

From there the views are magnificent, especially on clear days when no marine layer of clouds is present to the west.

For a different return, you can have someone wait for you in the Palm

Springs Lower Tram Station, and take the left fork trail down to the tram at Wellman Divide. This "short version" saves you almost 3 miles versus the same-way return to Humber Park and Idyllwild.

With over 120 established routes, Lily Rock attracts rock climbers from all over

44 South Ridge Trail to Tahquitz Peak Overlook *(see map on page 88)*

LENGTH: 7 miles	**SEASON:** May to November
HIKING TIME: 4 hours	**INFORMATION:** USDA Forest
ELEVATION GAIN: 2,000 feet	Service, Idyllwild, (909) 659-2117
DIFFICULTY: Strenuous	

The South Ridge Trail offers the hiker access to the higher southerly elevations of the great granite massif of San Jacinto Mountain. This steep trail takes you quickly through Jeffrey pine, live oak, and white fir to the more numerous lodgepole pine around Tahquitz Peak. The views, however, are the real treat. Along the way, the entire vista of the Desert Divide and Pacific Crest Trail, which form the eastern flank of the San Jacinto Mountains, can be seen. To the north, the hiker sees Marion Mountain surrounded by its granite crags. This trail is steep in places and demands that the hiker be in good aerobic condition.

Tahquitz Peak and Lily Rock

DIRECTIONS

This trail requires a wilderness permit from the Forest Service Office in Idyllwild and is reached by driving on Hwy. 74 south from Hwy. 111 in Palm Desert, turning right on Hwy. 243 at Mountain Center and proceeding about 4 miles to Saunders Meadow Road. From I-10 in Banning, take Hwy. 243 to Idyllwild and proceed south out of town until you come to this same road. Turn onto Saunders Meadow Road, then left on Pine Street for 0.25 mile, then right on Tahquitz View Drive for about 0.75 mile. You will then come to the base of South Ridge Road to the right. If you have a 4WD vehicle, proceed up the road for 1.5 miles to the trailhead; otherwise walk up to avoid the deep potholes and washouts if the winter has been severe.

Once at the trailhead, you will begin a steep climb that quickly offers you those great views. After a mile you'll be able to see Garner Valley, Thomas Mountain, and Lake Hemet to the south. A little farther up, the full glory of the Desert Divide Ridge is revealed to the east. Many hikers photograph themselves at a unique "window rock" found 1.5 miles up the trail which frames the wild granite crags to the north. The trail steeply switchbacks up to Tahquitz Peak Lookout Tower, offering you a 360 degree sweep of all the mountains in this area.

45 *Deer Springs Trail to Saddle Junction/ Humber Park* (see map on page 88)

LENGTH: 12 miles

HIKING TIME: 7 hours

ELEVATION GAIN: 3,300 feet

DIFFICULTY: Strenuous

SEASON: May to November

INFORMATION: USDA Forest Service, Idyllwild, (909) 659-2117

The Deer Springs Trail offers a vista-filled hike up San Jacinto Mountain's southwest flank, connecting to the Pacific Crest Trail (PCT) before descending along a lengthy ridge to Saddle Junction and finally to Humber Park Trailhead. The views from the ridge above Idyllwild are memorable, with the massive granite Tahquitz Ridge and Lily Rock filling the southeast horizon. This is a shuttle hike requiring hikers to park cars at both the Humber Park Trailhead (Devil's Slide Trail) and Deer Springs. The late summer weather can be tricky. The last time I did this hike we began in 80 degree temperatures and ended with a torrential downpour accompanied by hail.

DIRECTIONS To reach the trailhead for Deer Springs, take Hwy. 243 west of Idyllwild for 1 mile, and park on the left at the Idyllwild County Park Visitor's Center. The trail begins across the street at the wooden sign.

For the first 4.1 miles, you will climb through Jeffrey pine, oak, and manzanita. Looking west you will see the Hemet Valley and Santa Ana Mountains . . . on a smog free day, that is! You'll then intersect the PCT, which you'll take up to the ridge. Along the way you are treated to beautiful views, an occasional running spring, and an excellent chance to see wildflowers, especially Indian paintbrush.

After 8.3 miles you will arrive at Saddle Junction for your 2.5-mile descent to Humber Park. If you are shuttling, remember that on summer weekends and holidays, the Humber Park area can be filled with cars by mid morning; also, a day-hike permit is required.

The impressive Lily Rock as viewed from Devil's Slide Trailhead

46 *Deer Springs Trail to Suicide Rock*

(see map on page 88)

LENGTH: 7 miles

HIKING TIME: 3 – 4 hours

ELEVATION GAIN: 1,400 feet

DIFFICULTY: Moderate

SEASON: May to November

INFORMATION: USDA Forest Service, Idyllwild, (909) 659-2117

This hike is especially beautiful when winter snows have melted enough to allow a clear trail to the summit of Suicide Rock, or there are 6 inches or less on the trail at the base of Suicide Rock.

DIRECTIONS Follow the directions for Hike 45.

After parking at the trailhead, walk across Hwy. 243 to access the beginning of the hike. Deer Springs Trail leads through chaparral of manzanita and ribbonwood, pine, and low brush. In a wet winter this trail is best done in May-June, as several good streams cross or run alongside the trail and thick moss sometimes can blanket rocks where the runoff is generous. The trail climbs quickly toward the junction with the side trail that leads to Suicide Rock after 2.3 miles. At this point the ponderosa pine are large and dominant. At the junction turn right, noting Tahquitz Peak as the tallest mountain to the east across the valley, and Lily Rock—a rock formation that lures many climbers on any summer weekend—as a prominent granite formation down and to the left of Tahquitz Peak.

After turning right onto the trail to Suicide Rock, you are treated to vistas of Garner Valley and Thomas Mountain to the southeast and open horizons of the Santa Ana Mountains to the west. The trail encounters a fast-running stream, which drops down across the trail, and large scattered pines near Suicide Rock.

The last 0.25 mile climbs to Suicide Rock, where you must negotiate large boulders to gain the "summit." You will enjoy 360 degree views of the lands south and west of Idyllwild.

Indian paintbrush dots the terrain in the San Jacinto Mountains

47 *Hurkey Creek Trail*

LENGTH: 3 miles

HIKING TIME: 2 hours

ELEVATION GAIN: 300 feet

DIFFICULTY: Easy

SEASON: May to November

INFORMATION: Hurkey Creek Campground, Hurkey Creek (909) 659-2050

South of the Desert Divide Ridge and the Pacific Crest Trail in Apple Canyon, the mountains slope down and across a valley to reach over to Thomas Mountain. Hurkey Creek drains this area, and a county-run campground can be accessed for reservations from April 1 to October 21. The area around Hurkey Creek is quiet and scenic and offers a convenient campsite for those coming from either the Coachella Valley or metropolitan Los Angeles. A short but very scenic trail winds its way out of the campground and into the surrounding higher elevations. For day hikers wanting an easy hike, this trail fits the bill. From May to early June, flowers are in bloom along its path, and gentle vistas of the surrounding mountains complement the simplicity of this trail.

DIRECTIONS

To reach the trail and campground, drive on Hwy. 74 out of Hemet, to almost 4 miles past the junction of Mountain Center and Hwy. 243, or drive south on Hwy. 74, 32 miles from Hwy. 111 in Palm Desert. At Apple Canyon Road, across from Lake Hemet, turn north and then take a sharp left into the campground. The trail begins at the far west/southwest part of the campground.

Grazing horses at pasture in the Garner Valley

In early spring, be prepared for water and runoff spilling across and along-side the trail. The hike follows a wide dirt trail, climbs onto a nearby plateau and, if the brush has been cleared, leads back into the campground. Most hikers prefer to walk to the scenic open spaces, admire the view, and smell the flowers before turning back.

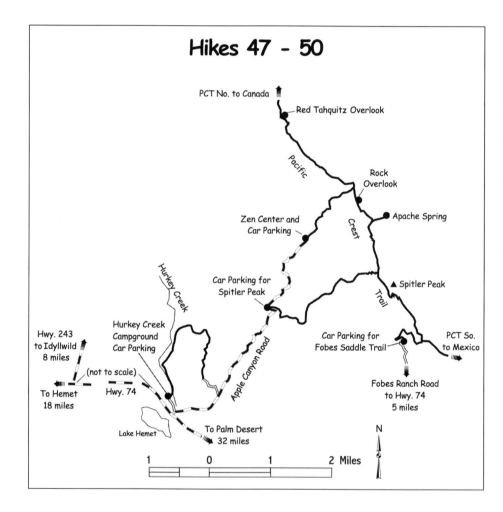

Hikes 47 - 50

PCT No. to Canada

Red Tahquitz Overlook

Rock Overlook

Apache Spring

Zen Center and Car Parking

Pacific

Crest

Hurkey Creek

Car Parking for Spitler Peak

Spitler Peak

Trail

Hurkey Creek Campground Car Parking

Hwy. 243 to Idyllwild 8 miles

Car Parking for Fobes Saddle Trail

PCT So. to Mexico

(not to scale)

To Hemet 18 miles

Hwy. 74

Apple Canyon Road

Fobes Ranch Road to Hwy. 74 5 miles

Lake Hemet

To Palm Desert 32 miles

N

1   0   1   2 Miles

48 Fobes Saddle to Spitler Peak and Apache Spring

LENGTH: 6 miles

HIKING TIME: 4 hours

ELEVATION GAIN: 1,800 feet

DIFFICULTY: Strenuous

SEASON: March to December

INFORMATION: USDA Forest Service, Idyllwild, (909) 659-2117

The advantage of the Fobes Saddle Trail is the quick access it gives the hiker to the Pacific Crest Trail (PCT). This section of the PCT/Desert Divide is known for its ruggedness, chaparral, and scrub brush and continues to take the hiker closer to the large mass of San Jacinto Mountain.

DIRECTIONS

To get to the trailhead, take Hwy. 74 south from Palm Desert for almost 30 miles. After passing Morris Ranch Road, begin looking to the right for the large sign indicating Fobes Saddle Trail. The entry past the sign is through a metal gate left open during the day. This road to Fobes Saddle Trailhead is not paved and is more safely done by a 4WD vehicle. If the winter was particularly rainy, expect sizable potholes, washouts, and rough conditions. For these reasons, this trail is not nearly as popular as the Cedar Spring PCT access at Morris Ranch.

The trail begins after a 3-mile drive down the dirt road. There is a very fast switchback of 0.75 mile up to the ridge and the PCT. Turn left and up the mountain through brush and forest thickets. If the trail has not been well maintained, you will find the going slow. The views of the Coachella Valley are beautiful but the vegetation is more wilderness scrub. Continue for almost 2 miles to Spitler Peak, which rises above you to the south. After the peak, continue west until you see the sign for Apache Spring, a 500-foot descent down the mountain. If the winter snow has been heavy, this section might have several feet of snow for you to contend with.

49 The Zen Center to Red Tahquitz Overlook (see map on page 102)

LENGTH: 12 miles

HIKING TIME: 7 hours

ELEVATION GAIN: 2,500 feet

DIFFICULTY: Strenuous

SEASON: May to November

INFORMATION: USDA Forest Service, Idyllwild, (909) 659-2117

There are vista hikes all along the Pacific Crest Trail (PCT) ridge of the San Jacinto Mountains. However, this section of trail has many a hiker's vote for being the most scenic and spectacular. It is one of the favorite hikes of the Coachella Valley Hiking Club and offers a stunning variety of vistas and terrain. The trail is not on many maps because the first section of the trail begins on private property at the Zen Center east of Idyllwild. The Zen Master in residence allows hikers to use this trail but with several cautions. Bring as few vehicles as possible. Hike quietly for the first 0.5 mile, to avoid disturbing the meditation and tranquility of those staying at the Center. Keep groups small, and no dogs are allowed.

DIRECTIONS

To reach the trailhead, drive 3.5 miles east of the Hwy. 74/Mountain Center junction, or approximately 33 miles south of Palm Desert on Hwy. 74. Turn onto Apple Canyon Road and continue almost 4 miles until you reach the large Retreat Center, which looks like a hotel. Drive down the dirt road—found to the right of where the paved road ends and next to a small fence—until you reach the Zen Center. Park in the small dirt area just before entering the grounds.

The trail begins north of the parking area and meanders through the center's scattering of cottages and trailers. Cairns mark the trail. You continue this way for almost 0.5 mile until the trail appears to end in a grove of beautiful incense cedar, converging along a quiet stream. Look up and to the left to find the trail marked as it begins climbing the hillside through thickets of bush, pine, yucca, and manzanita. Keep a sharp eye out for the trail, as it seems to sometimes merge into other side trails.

The ascent up the mountain is a steep 1,200-foot gain in just over a mile. Be careful of the cacti and slippery trail conditions. Once at the top, to the right you will find a log resting place for a well-deserved break. The trail intersects the PCT a few feet north of the logs. Although the day's hike is to the west, take the trail to the right (east) for 0.5 mile up and alongside the mountain. This section is highlighted by awesome sheer drops into steep rocky canyons and colorful rock formations. You will finally turn a corner and see a 200-yard rock overlook to your left. Hike out to the end for the most awesome views of this entire desert and mountain region. Return to where the trail heads west from the log rest stop. You are treated along the way to splendid canyon views of West Fork and Murray canyons, rising steeply out of Palm Canyon below.

The trail is an adventurous hike beneath the ridge of the mountain and sometimes actually reaches the crest from which you can see toward San Diego and the Pacific Ocean. The magnificence of the views along this hike cannot be overstated. They will make you feel happy to be alive and glad you took up hiking! There is an exhilarating feeling of openness all during the hike. As you head ever closer to the view of Red Tahquitz and massive San Jacinto Mountain, you can look down the entire length of the Salton Sea, accented by the equally exciting view of the mountain ranges which extend to the Anza-Borrego Desert.

The hike ends when you come to a granite saddle from which Red Tahquitz Peak looks so very close but is still many miles of strenuous hiking away. If you have the stamina you can continue to Red Tahquitz. The return hike gives you miles of great vistas all the way from where the trail starts down to the Zen Center. Here, be very careful. The trail is steep and the footing is slippery. Remember to observe silence or at least quiet conversation as you approach the Zen Center.

With its steep cliff exposure, the Zen Center Trail definitely qualifies as a strenuous hike

50 *Spitler Peak Trail*
(see map on page 102)

LENGTH: 10 miles

HIKING TIME: 6 hours

ELEVATION GAIN: 2,000 feet

DIFFICULTY: Strenuous

SEASON: Year-round

INFORMATION: USDA Forest Service, Idyllwild, (909) 659-2117

This trail to Spitler Peak is the most direct route up the mountain, allowing the hiker to avoid lengthy sections of the Pacific Crest Trail (PCT) in an attempt to reach the peak. The views at the top show the panorama of the Santa Rosa and San Jacinto mountains with glimpses of the Palomar Range to the south.

DIRECTIONS

Reach the trailhead by following the directions for Hike 49. Drive 33 miles south of Palm Desert on Hwy. 74. Turn right on Apple Canyon Road (3.5 miles east of Mountain Center). At nearly 3 miles you will see the sign for the Spitler Peak Trail on the road's right shoulder. Park here and begin the climb to the peak.

The trail winds steeply up through manzanita and other chaparral brush. If the trail has been properly maintained, as it usually is, the ascent up the slope is relatively unimpeded. Once at the top, you can choose to head either east toward Fobes Saddle and down to the trailhead, or west to where the PCT meets the Zen Center Trail. Either way, you must arrange a shuttle. Each of these hikes is close to 8 miles long and is described elsewhere in this book. The trail to Spitler Peak is a short 0.5 mile from where the PCT meets the trail coming up from the trailhead.

The San Jacinto Mountains are easily viewed from the Pacific Crest Trail

51 Ramona Trail to Tool Box Spring

LENGTH: 11 miles

HIKING TIME: 6 hours

ELEVATION GAIN: 2,000 feet

DIFFICULTY: Strenuous

SEASON: Year-round

INFORMATION: USDA Forest Service, Idyllwild, (909) 659-2117

South of the San Jacinto Mountains rises the much smaller Thomas Mountain. This mountain forms the southern border for the intervening Garner Valley. There are few trails on this mountain, the San Jacintos having captured the lion's share with the Pacific Crest Trail and Desert Divide Ridge. Still, the beautiful trail to the top of Thomas Mountain via Tool Box Spring is worth the effort.

DIRECTIONS

To reach this trailhead, travel 8 miles east from the junction of Hwy. 243 and 74, staying on Hwy. 74 until you see the trailhead sign to your right. From Palm Desert, take Hwy. 74 south almost 28 miles and look for the trail sign to your left indicating Thomas Mountain.

Access the trail by walking along the dirt road, passing through a gate, then taking the trail on the left side of the road as it begins its switchback up the mountain. As is common to these mountains, you will hike through thick outgrowths of manzanita, ribbonwood, and sage. Manzanita is the smooth bush with dark red bark that is often mistaken for ribbonwood, which has ribbonlike bark hanging as streamers.

After almost 3 miles you will arrive at Tool Box Spring, where a dirt road joins with the trail. Continue for another 1.5 miles west along the mountain ridge to a junction where you can turn left for the 0.5-mile ascent of Thomas Mountain.

The views at the top are of Anza Valley to the south and the San Jacinto Mountains to the north, with Garner Valley in between. This trail can be hot in the summer, depending on whether cool ocean breezes are blowing onshore from the Pacific.

This campground at Tool Box Spring provides a great resting spot for hikers

Hikes 51 - 53

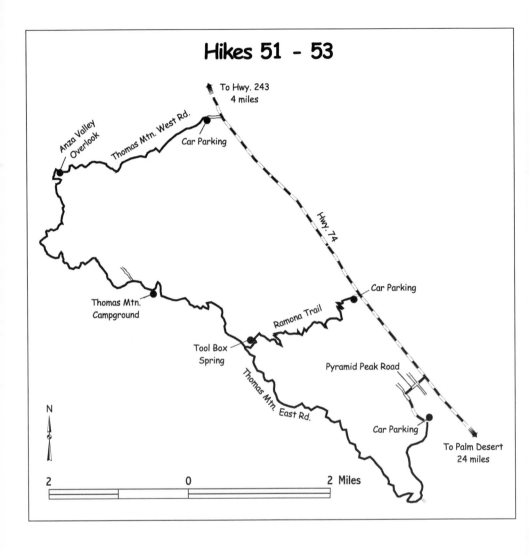

To Hwy. 243
4 miles

Anza Valley
Overlook

Thomas Mtn. West Rd.

Car Parking

Hwy. 74

Car Parking

Thomas Mtn.
Campground

Ramona Trail

Tool Box
Spring

Pyramid Peak Road

Thomas Mtn. East Rd.

Car Parking

To Palm Desert
24 miles

N

2   0   2 Miles

52 *Thomas Mountain East Road to Summit*

LENGTH: 10 – 12 miles

HIKING TIME: 6 hours

ELEVATION GAIN: 2,000 feet

DIFFICULTY: Moderate/strenuous

SEASON: Year-round

INFORMATION: USDA Forest Service, Idyllwild, (909) 659-2117

This hike offers spectacular views of the Anza Valley to the south and the San Jacinto Mountains/Desert Divide Ridge—along which the Pacific Crest Trail follows—to the north. The top of Thomas Mountain is well forested with ponderosa pine and gives cool relief to desert hikers from late spring through early fall. Restrooms and picnic tables complete the amenities, but the real reward is a scenic, gently graded trail that is more moderate than strenuous.

DIRECTIONS

From Hwy. 111 in Palm Desert, turn south onto Hwy. 74 and proceed for 24 miles until you pass Hwy. 371 to San Diego. Stay on Hwy. 74 for 3 miles past the 371 cutoff. Look to the left for Pyramid Peak Road with a brown sign indicating Thomas Mountain (6s13). Turn left down Pyramid Peak Road until it dead-ends at the stop sign. Then turn left at Hop Patch Springs Road and continue for another mile until the road changes from paved to dirt. Park where convenient. A National Forest Adventure Pass (NFAP) is required for parking. If you're coming from Hemet, Pyramid Peak Road is almost 9 miles from Mountain Center on the right.

After parking, begin the gentle hike up this dirt road, being watchful for any vehicles coming down the mountain. The drivers often do not expect hikers,

so give them ample road space. The first 0.5 mile features ponderosa pine, but soon the vegetation thins out into high chaparral, with a bias toward ribbonwood. If the winter rains have been generous, this trail will yield a rich array of wildflowers and flowering bushes in late

High chaparral along Thomas Mountain East Road

March through May. It's best to do this hike in the early morning to smell the
sage and other flowering plants while the air is still cool and moist.

The first section of the hike reminds me of the Hill Country near Austin,
Texas, and offers pastoral views of the valley to the south. After almost 3 miles
the views begin to favor the San Jacinto Mountains to the north. If winter snow
is abundant on this range, the view in early spring can be stunning. The hike
continues past a cow grating where cows may be grazing. Quickly and quietly
pass by, and continue up the mountain, turning back often to see the Anza-
Borrego Desert far to the southeast.

After almost 5 miles you will enter the thickly forested area at the top of
Thomas Mountain. Restrooms soon come into view, along with picnic tables.
You can continue on this trail and see beautiful pine forests, turning back and
returning down the same trail whenever you feel that you've gone far enough.
This trail is delightful in any season, offering great vistas to the north and south,
as well as Garner Valley lying between Thomas Mountain and the San Jacinto
Mountains to the north.

53 *Thomas Mountain West Road to Anza Valley Overlook* (see map on page 108)

LENGTH: 10 miles

HIKING TIME: 4 – 5 hours

ELEVATION GAIN: 2,000 feet

DIFFICULTY: Moderate/strenuous

SEASON: Year-round

INFORMATION: USDA Forest
Service, Idyllwild, (909) 659-2117

*This hike completes the trio of hikes on Thomas Mountain (see also Hikes 51 and 52)
and offers spectacular vistas of Lake Hemet early on, the San Jacinto Mountains to
the north, the Santa Ana Mountains to the west, and the expansive Anza Valley to
the south.*

DIRECTIONS

Follow the directions for Hike 52, but after driving 27 miles from
Hwy. 111 in Palm Desert, continue another 4.5 miles until you see
on your right the brown sign indicating Thomas Mountain Road.
This road is just east of Lake Hemet by almost a mile. Turn off
Hwy. 74 and park where convenient. Like all trails in the Santa Rosa/
San Jacinto Mountains, this trail requires a National Forest Adventure
Pass (NFAP).

After parking, begin this hike on the western side of Thomas Mountain, climbing to the top by following the dirt road you drove in on. After 0.75 mile, you can see Lake Hemet below you. This hike is especially scenic in spring (April or May), depending on what kind of winter it has been and how much rain has fallen. Abundant flowers fill the green, grassy fields and pastureland of Garner Valley to the north if rainfall has been adequate. Depending on the year, small pestering flies can be a nuisance.

After 3 miles the trail begins to access the denser forested areas. Views of Anza Valley soon greet you looking south, while the mountains east of Hemet rise to the west. If you continue 5 miles from the trailhead, you will be hiking on the south side of Thomas Mountain with Anza Valley dominating your view. However, another 0.75 mile will lead you into the thick pine forest at the top. This is a good turn-around spot; or if you want to push it, continue for another mile to see the east-facing view of the mountain. If your party is large enough, you can make a 13-mile shuttle hike one-way by parking vehicles at the trail ends of both East and West Thomas Mountain roads, exchanging car keys along

the way. This hike makes for a great full moon ramble in spring or fall, with views of Lake Hemet shimmering beneath you for the first 1.5 miles.

Looking back, hikers get a great view of Garner Valley

54 Seven Pines Trail to Marion Mountain Camp

LENGTH: 6.5 miles

HIKING TIME: 5 hours

ELEVATION GAIN: 2,300 feet

DIFFICULTY: Strenuous

SEASON: May to October

INFORMATION: USDA Forest Service, Idyllwild, (909) 659-2117

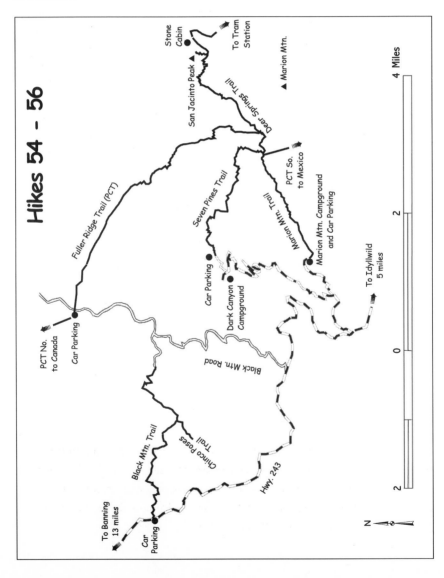

This is a shuttle hike and one of the few hikes in the San Jacinto Mountains which travels alongside a river. This trip gives the hiker great views of Fuller Ridge to the north, Hemet Valley to the west, and the cooler western side of the San Jacinto Mountains. Cars need to be parked at both the Seven Pines Trailhead and the Marion Mountain Trailhead.

DIRECTIONS From the U.S. Forest Service Office in Idyllwild, take Hwy. 243, going 5 miles west to the Allandale station. Turn right for the Marion Mountain Campground and park at the trailhead just before the campground. Take the other cars back toward Hwy. 243 but turn right before reaching the highway at the sign for Dark Canyon Campground. Continue through the campground and up the hill until you reach the trailhead for Seven Pines.

This trail climbs swiftly up through forest and granite boulders, with the looming, craggy wall of Fuller Ridge dominating the northern horizon. After more than a mile you are treated to the beautiful North Fork of the San Jacinto River. The trail crosses it through a magnificent grove of incense cedar and other pines. This makes a good rest stop and is so beautifully serene that it tempts hikers to go no farther. For this reason the short hike to the river makes a perfect summer picnic outing.

Hardier souls (and remember, you parked the cars at the other trailhead) push on and upward through more lush pines and boulder outcroppings. As you climb the 2,300 feet to the junction of Marion Mountain, you crisscross a series of gullies. The trail, unfortunately, has been badly eroded from past runoffs and can be quite rocky and steep in places.

Once you reach the Marion Mountain Trail, turn right and down the mountain for the 2.5-mile trek back to your vehicles. The views will continue to amaze you, but this section of trail is especially steep, with many sections burdened by 2-foot drop-offs. Those who have done this loop prefer to travel up the river-and-fern canyons of Seven Pines Trail to avoid having to haul themselves up the steeper Marion Mountain Trail.

Many hikers are captivated by the beauty of Dark Canyon Campground, which they must pass through to reach the Seven Pines Trailhead. The "dark" refers to the generous population of incense cedar and other thickets of pine that make this campground a welcome relief from the hotter lowlands surrounding San Jacinto Mountain.

55 *Fuller Ridge Trail to San Jacinto Peak*

(see map on page 112)

LENGTH: 15 miles

HIKING TIME: 10 hours

ELEVATION GAIN: 3,200 feet

DIFFICULTY: Strenuous

SEASON: June to November

INFORMATION: USDA Forest Service, Idyllwild, (909) 659-2117

As visitors to the Coachella Valley drive through the San Gorgonio Pass near Cabazon, they can look south to San Jacinto Peak and see a massive granite ridge emerging from the heights above the north face of San Jacinto Mountain and thrusting westward before descending sharply to the foothills beyond. This is the rugged Fuller Ridge and along its granite mass runs the Pacific Crest Trail, known through this section as the Fuller Ridge Trail. The views from near the top are magnificent, high-lighting the San Gorgonio Mountains and peak to the north, and the spreading deserts stretching like a carpet between the two mountain ranges. This demanding hike and its weather can be tricky. A hike has been known to begin at 7 a.m. with 40 degree temperatures, only to end the day in the high 80s. The ascent to San Jacinto Peak further tests your endurance, but is worth the additional effort!

DIRECTIONS

To reach the trailhead, drive 7 miles north from Idyllwild on Hwy. 243 or 17 miles south from Banning on Hwy. 243. Go east on Black Mountain Road almost 8 miles to the trailhead and park. This road can be quite rough on anything but a 4WD vehicle, so plan accordingly.

Snow often persists on San Jacinto's nearly 11,000-foot peaks through June, when the temperature 10 miles away on the valley floor may be well over 100 degrees

From the trailhead you quickly climb to where granite outcroppings abound and the views begin to spread your horizon in all directions. After 3 to 4 miles you can look down the north face of San Jacinto Mountain into the plunging granite abyss of Snow Creek Gorge . . . this dropview alone is worth the hike! The ridge travels up and down, climbing relentlessly through pine, cedar, and fir until after 5 miles the trail joins with the Deer Springs Trail. From here, turn left and proceed for 2.6 miles up to the peak of San Jacinto Mountain before returning. An easier but more logistically difficult feat is to have someone drop your group off at the Fuller Ridge Trailhead, and instead of backtracking, you can continue down the eastern side of the mountain to the Mountain Tram Station and take the tram into Palm Springs before being picked up. This will shave almost 3 miles off the hike and about 1,000 feet of additional climbing.

56 *Black Mountain Trail*
(see map on page 112)

LENGTH: 7 miles	**SEASON:** Year-round
HIKING TIME: 4 hours	**INFORMATION:** USDA Forest
ELEVATION GAIN: 2,600 feet	Service, Idyllwild, (909) 659-2117
DIFFICULTY: Strenuous	

Tahquitz Peak

This trail climbs up Black Mountain to give the hiker superb views of the desert valleys below, and Banning Pass and the San Gorgonio Mountains to the north. Black Mountain is the northernmost peak in the San Jacinto Range, and one of the first hikes along the Banning–Idyllwild Road.

DIRECTIONS

To reach the trail, drive south from Banning on Hwy. 243 for 13 miles until you reach Black Mountain Trail, just 1.25 miles past the Vista Grande Ranger Station.

The trail winds through a burned area left from the Soboba fire in 1974, with some charred remains still visible. After 2.5 miles you will meet the Chinco Poses Trail, where'll you continue left up the mountain before reaching the Black Mountain Lookout Road. From here, hike the remaining distance to the lookout tower for sweeping views before returning to your starting point.

This trail can be cooler than you might expect in summer if onshore Pacific breezes are blowing that day. For this reason, this trail is a favorite with desert hikers seeking to cool off without driving all the way to Idyllwild.

57 *North Fork of the Pacific Crest Trail to Live Oak Spring*

LENGTH: 14 miles

HIKING TIME: 8 hours

ELEVATION GAIN: 2,000 feet

DIFFICULTY: Strenuous

SEASON: Year-round

INFORMATION: USDA Forest Service, Idyllwild, (909) 659-2117

The North Fork of the Pacific Crest Trail (PCT) offers the hiker a scenic, meandering, gradual climb to the Desert Divide Ridge overlooking the Coachella Valley with the added treat of visiting a beautiful grove of massive oak trees surrounded by grassy meadows and vine thickets, all fed by the rushing waters of Live Oak Spring. The Desert Divide Ridge is accompanied all the way to Idyllwild by the PCT. It offers a cool escape from the sweltering desert below and stunning vistas of the Coachella Valley; Santa Rosa and San Jacinto mountain ranges; and the Salton Sea Basin on the eastern horizon.

DIRECTIONS

The trailhead directions are the same as for the South Fork PCT (Hike 68), taking Hwy. 74 from Palm Desert 23 miles to the parking area, or 0.5 mile east of the Hwy. 371 junction.

Hikes 57 - 61

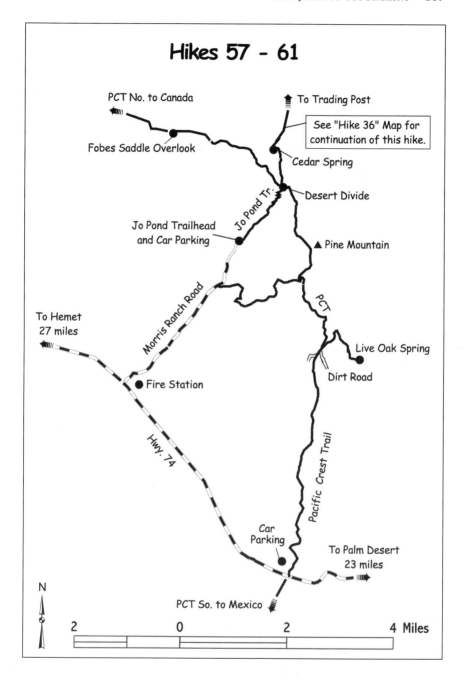

PCT No. to Canada

To Trading Post

See "Hike 36" Map for continuation of this hike.

Fobes Saddle Overlook

Cedar Spring

Jo Pond Tr.

Desert Divide

Jo Pond Trailhead and Car Parking

Pine Mountain

Morris Ranch Road

PCT

To Hemet 27 miles

Live Oak Spring

Fire Station

Dirt Road

Hwy. 74

Pacific Crest Trail

Car Parking

To Palm Desert 23 miles

PCT So. to Mexico

N

2   0   2   4 Miles

The trail begins with a massive mileage sign and description of the PCT system found in this area. The trail winds slowly down a hillside covered with manzanita, yucca, juniper, and pine. Although the route doesn't offer spectacular vistas, the vegetation's scents are invigorating in the cool morning air. The trail makes its way into a boulder area for several miles, then climbs alongside a low mountain. The views reveal working ranches below, as well as the Mount Palomar Observatory to the southwest. You will pass through a variety of pine and high-desert scrub brush, with some small streams running from January to March.

After 5 miles the trail crosses a small dirt road. Look for the rock ducks that indicate the trail continues on the other side of this road. You will now hug a rocky mountainside for the last mile before reaching the top of the trail at Desert Divide. This is exactly 6 miles from where you began. Continue down for another mile to Live Oak Spring. The spring area offers a quiet, green lunch stop. It reminds many hikers of the oak-covered hillsides in Northern California. The two oak tree systems found at Live Oak Spring are massive because of the perpetual source of running water. If you continued 5 miles down the mountain you would intersect Palm Canyon.

Take care to carry enough cold water. In these parts you often begin a hike with cool temperatures but end the afternoon pushing 90 to 100 degrees.

58 *North Fork of the Pacific Crest Trail to Jo Pond Trailhead* (see map on page 117)

LENGTH: 14 miles

HIKING TIME: 5 – 6 hours

ELEVATION GAIN: 1,700 feet

DIFFICULTY: Strenuous

SEASON: March to November

INFORMATION: USDA Forest Service, Idyllwild, (909) 659-2117

This loop hike takes you up to the Pacific Crest Trail (PCT), west along the spine of the Desert Divide section of the San Jacinto Mountains, then back down the mountain for a scenic hike offering spectacular vistas of the Coachella Valley, Thomas Mountain, the Palomar Mountains, and the Santa Rosas.

DIRECTIONS   Park vehicles at the trailheads for Hikes 57 and 60.

Begin by hiking the North Fork of the PCT, heading north toward the San Jacinto Mountains. The hike first rambles through thick chaparral along a winding hillside dominated by ribbonwood and manzanita, with a scattering of pinyon pine. After 2 miles you will begin to climb into a rocky area, and then for the next 1.5 miles you'll make your way through granite/sand composite rock fields with views toward the west. The trail then drops down onto a flat area before again climbing up the hillside to the east. After another 2.5 miles you will reach a gate where you must turn left up the mountain in order to stay on the PCT.

The trail heads west on top of the mountain until reaching the area near Pine Mountain. Here the trail climbs up the mountainside, tops along the mountain,

crests again, then connects with the Jo Pond Trail after 2 miles. At this junction, turn left southward down the mountain and hike 2 miles until returning to where your vehicle is parked at the Jo Pond Trailhead.

Markers along the Pacific Crest Trail help guide hikers in the right direction

59 *Jo Pond Trail and Pine Mountain Loop*

(see map on page 117)

LENGTH: 10 – 11 miles

HIKING TIME: 5 hours

ELEVATION GAIN: 1,500 feet

DIFFICULTY: Strenuous

SEASON: March to November

INFORMATION: USDA Forest Service, Idyllwild, (909) 659-2117

If you do this hike with more than one vehicle, park one car at the Jo Pond Trailhead parking area, and the other 1 mile farther south on Morris Ranch Road, just across or next to the county road marked by a wooden sign on the right as you drive in. This shuttle cuts the hike's length from 11 to 10 miles and avoids a return walking on the pavement.

DIRECTIONS   Follow the directions for Hike 60.

Some Pacific Crest Trail markers provide more than just directions

This hike allows you to access the Pacific Crest Trail (PCT) hike toward Pine Mountain (almost 7,000 feet high), and loop back to your parked cars. Begin by walking from your car 100 yards north to the sign for Cedar Spring. After passing through the gate, continue uphill for 0.25 mile until you come to the trail sign that shows a left turn and takes you into a thicket of oak trees. The trail soon meets the Jo Pond Trailhead sign, and you will follow along a flowing stream if winter rains were generous enough. Along this trail section I've actually seen bobcat. The trail soon passes through another gate, over a meadow area made especially beautiful in spring and fall by appropriate colors and flowers, and up to yet another trail sign.

From here the trail makes its last touch with green undergrowth before climbing the high hillside for a 1,200-foot elevation gain over 1.5 miles. At the top of the mountain the trail joins with the PCT. Explore for a few minutes the Cedar Spring section going down the other side toward the Coachella Valley for some great vistas, then return to where you meet the PCT at the top and turn east. For the next several miles the trail offers you spectacular views of the surrounding mountains, valleys, and the San Jacinto Range upon which you are hiking. Eventually the trail follows a sharp turn south toward some small peaks. Note the peak due east, with large rocks scattered about its flank; this is Pine Mountain.

The trail then drops down the other side of the mountain, cutting down the wind on a windy day, before meeting up with a wide dirt road trail at a small saddle. To the left you can plainly see the trail heading toward Pine Mountain, but do not travel left. Rather, when you join this wider trail, turn right through a fence post area, and continue on this trail section as it takes you through a scenic area marked by grasslands and pine trees.

This section offers stunning views of the spine of the mountain heading southeast, reminding many of the Blue Ridge Mountains. The trail will gradually turn down and veer right to a major trail split. Turn right or westerly here, and follow the trail past more pine, a small reservoir, and the first indications of civilization. You will eventually come to a large gate; it either will be open or you must climb over. The Forest Service has informed me that this "trail" is open to hikers; it's just not well marked as such.

The trail continues down and up over small hills, eventually skirting a Girl Scout camp development before finally returning to Morris Ranch Road.

The views and quiet scenery along the way are well worth the effort, especially the swing down the mountain with the cool pine forests and fragrant smells having a magical impact in April-May.

60 *Jo Pond Trail to Cedar Spring*
(see map on page 117)

LENGTH: 7 miles

HIKING TIME: 4 hours

ELEVATION GAIN: 1,700 feet

DIFFICULTY: Moderate

SEASON: Year-round

INFORMATION: USDA Forest Service, Idyllwild, (909) 659-2117

In 1994 the Jo Pond Trail connecting Palm Canyon in Palm Springs to the south terminus at the Cedar Spring Trailhead was completed. This magnificent 13-mile trail allows hikers to climb either the Pacific Crest Trail (PCT) in the San Jacinto Mountains at Desert Divide and drop down into Palm Canyon along the West Fork Trail, or to reverse direction. Hikers need to arrange a car shuttle at either end, have someone drop them off and pick them up when finished, or have two groups hike in opposite directions and exchange car keys. The best times of the year are late October to late November and from mid-winter to April. The Jo Pond Trail treats the hiker to spectacular vistas of the Coachella Valley and surrounding mountains and, like its cousin the Pines-to-Palms Trail, provides a variety of desert and mountain flora to enjoy along the way.

DIRECTIONS

To reach the south terminus trailhead for the Cedar Spring section, take Hwy. 74 south from Palm Desert off Hwy. 111, driving 28 miles to Morris Ranch Road in Garner Valley. Turn right at the fire station and continue 3.5 miles to where the road ends and a sign indicates to park off-pavement.

Park here and follow the road, on foot, for 100 yards until you see the sign for the Cedar Spring Trail. Within minutes you will be walking along a delightful stream in a grove of beautiful oak, provided you hike sometime between January and April. You will soon see the large sign indicating the Jo Pond Trail with mileage to various highlights along the way. The trail continues through a meadow, green and well flowered from April to May, then climbs for 1.5 miles up a series of switchbacks until reaching the top of the PCT at Desert Divide. This first 3-mile section can be very hot during the late spring through summer. Hikers need to assess whether a Pacific onshore breeze is blowing. During these times it can be 110 in the desert below, but 65 degrees on this section of the trail. Also, watch for ticks.

Hikers have several options when they reach the top of the crest. I suggest you first take the right fork to the east and explore for a mile or so; then return to the crest and continue down the desert side for 1 mile until you reach Cedar Spring. This is a beautiful lunch spot or rest area. Many hikers choose to camp

here before exploring nearby trails. You will find a generous number of incense cedar and black oak, with running water nearby. The return trip offers views of the Palomar Mountains to the south.

Winter comes to the Pacific Crest Trail above Cedar Spring

61 *Jo Pond Trail to Fobes Saddle Overlook*
(see map on page 117)

LENGTH: 9 miles

HIKING TIME: 5 hours

ELEVATION GAIN: 1,200 feet

DIFFICULTY: Moderate

SEASON: Year-round

INFORMATION: USDA Forest Service, Idyllwild, (909) 659-2117

DIRECTIONS   To reach the trailhead, follow the directions for Hike 60.

The Pacific Crest Trail (PCT), which follows the ridgeline of the San Jacinto Mountains, takes the hiker through many scenic sections that yield spectacular views of the Santa Rosa Mountains to the southeast and the San Jacinto Mountains as they run northwest and culminate at San Jacinto Peak. Always drawing the hiker's attention along this section is the Coachella Valley, which sprawls beneath the mountains and ends at the Salton Sea Basin. This grand vista hike — the PCT along the San Jacinto Range — also offers the hiker an opportunity to see terrain that suggests someplace other than the harsher desert conditions below. Valley residents can quickly escape by accessing the PCT at the Jo Pond Trailhead's south terminus and then can enjoy an invigorating hike through pine forests found by hiking west where the Jo Pond Trail intersects the Desert Divide. This section eventually takes you to an expansive overlook that shows the entire eastern flank of the San Jacinto Mountains.

Once you begin the hike it is 2.5 miles to the Desert Divide ridge and the PCT. Here, turn left up the mountain. As you climb, look often to the rear and take in the views of the many mountains due east — the Santa Rosas as well as Martinez Mountain. This section makes a marvelous "snow hike" from January to March. The snow is sometimes only 4 to 6 inches deep, but you will still come away feeling like you've experienced real winter conditions.

You will crest the mountain after only 0.5 mile. Beneath you is the long, thin trail of Palm Canyon coming out of Palm Springs to the north and ending in the Santa Rosa Mountains to the south. As you continue west you will be amazed

At 10,804 feet, San Jacinto Peak is the highest point in the San Jacinto Mountains

by the spectacular peak system of the San Jacintos, a feature that fills the entire western skyline. This view is made more beautiful if the winter snows have been generous. Hikers taking this trail in late October and early November are treated to the fall colors of the thick stands of oak found along the ridge.

After 1.5 miles along the ridge, you will come to a sign that indicates the trail going down into a thick pine forest. Before taking this trail, walk another 25 yards to the rocky point south of this sign. This makes a great lunch spot with magnificent views of the eastern flank of the San Jacinto Mountains. Continue through the pine forest and eventually you'll reach Fobes Saddle Overlook, which reveals the low saddle along the ridge trail as you look down and westward. The return hike treats you to more spectacular mountain vistas, with the Santa Rosa Mountains filling the eastern horizon.

Santa Rosa Mountains
Hikes 62 – 68

Trailhead Locations
in the Santa Rosa Mountains
(Hikes 62 - 68)

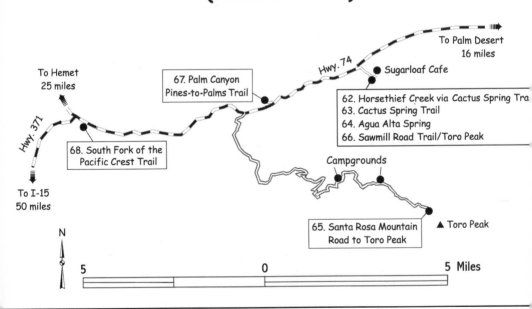

To Palm Desert
16 miles

To Hemet
25 miles

Hwy. 74

Sugarloaf Cafe

67. Palm Canyon
Pines-to-Palms Trail

62. Horsethief Creek via Cactus Spring Trail
63. Cactus Spring Trail
64. Agua Alta Spring
66. Sawmill Road Trail/Toro Peak

Hwy. 371

68. South Fork of the
Pacific Crest Trail

Campgrounds

To I-15
50 miles

65. Santa Rosa Mountain
Road to Toro Peak

▲ Toro Peak

N

5   0   5 Miles

62 *Horsethief Creek via Cactus Spring Trail*

LENGTH: 5 miles

HIKING TIME: 4 hours

ELEVATION GAIN: 900 feet

DIFFICULTY: Easy/moderate

SEASON: October to May

INFORMATION: USDA Forest Service, Idyllwild, (909) 659-2117

The Santa Rosa Mountain Wilderness area is a world apart from the desert surrounding it. This is a land of high chaparral, pinyon pine, yucca, juniper, agave, manzanita, ribbonwood, and prickly pear. The southern horizon is dominated by the twin massifs of Santa Rosa and Toro peaks, 8,000 and 8,700 feet high, while to the northwest the hiker can see the San Jacinto and San Gorgonio mountains filling up the sky. A favorite and easy way to explore this wild country is to hike the length of the Cactus Spring Trail, which penetrates deep into this wilderness area. The first segment of this hike is the beautiful Horsethief Creek section.

DIRECTIONS

To reach the trailhead, turn south from Hwy. 111 in Palm Desert onto Hwy. 74. Proceed up the mountain for almost 16 miles until you pass Sugarloaf Cafe, where you will take the first paved road to the left. A sign on Hwy. 74 indicates the Cactus Spring Trailhead. Go 0.25 mile, then turn left onto the wide dirt road. Park in the flat area north of the trash disposal. From Hemet, the trailhead is 8 miles east of the junction of Hwy. 371 and Hwy. 74.

After parking, hike east down the dirt road, then right (south) when you come to the larger dirt road heading up the mountain. After 100 yards you will see the Cactus Spring Trail sign to the left. Begin down the trail and be careful to turn, as it veers right after 0.25 mile. You will begin making your way through a thicket of vegetation, cacti, and pinyon pine. Within minutes the trail opens onto the remains of an abandoned dolomite mine. Continue east. The trail is a roller-coaster, up-and-down journey with a bias toward the down side. Be careful of fine loose rock when heading downhill. Sturdy hiking boots will help cushion this rocky trail.

As you head east, Martinez Mountain will fill the horizon. The trail is often washed by several streams, so you should be cautious of slippery rocks. By April, though, most of the streams have dried up. Hikers are often amazed by the large size of plants due to the abundant runoff during winter.

After more than 2 miles, look to your left, slightly downhill and off-trail, for the remains of an old corral made of dried manzanita. Cowboys once kept their herds penned here because of the water supply at Horsethief Creek.

The trail takes you to a rise above Horsethief Creek in a dramatic fashion. From this vantage point you can view the beautiful cottonwood and sycamore

trees lining the creek bed for the better part of a mile. In late October, the canyon creek area is ablaze with bright yellow—a scene one might expect more in Pennsylvania than California. Drop down into the creek and you can explore upstream for a mile, although there is no trail to lead you; just follow the water through thickets of vines, trees, and bushes. Many hikers come to Horsethief Creek for a reprieve from the sweltering desert heat below, and are well rewarded. After returning to their vehicles, some hikers opt for a visit to Sugarloaf Cafe, where they will find friendly service, good food, and a pleasant atmosphere.

A multitude of vegetation thrives along Horsethief Creek

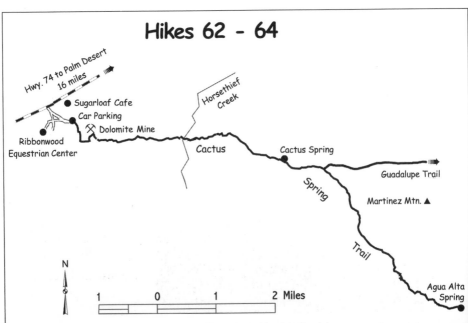

Hikes 62 - 64

Hwy. 74 to Palm Desert 16 miles

Sugarloaf Cafe
Car Parking
Dolomite Mine
Ribbonwood Equestrian Center

Horsethief Creek

Cactus

Cactus Spring

Spring

Guadalupe Trail

Martinez Mtn. ▲

Trail

Agua Alta Spring

N

1   0   1   2 Miles

63 *Cactus Spring Trail*

LENGTH: 9 miles

HIKING TIME: 5 hours

ELEVATION GAIN: 1,200 feet

DIFFICULTY: Moderate

SEASON: October to May

INFORMATION: USDA Forest Service, Idyllwild, (909) 659-2117

The trail to Cactus Spring brings the hiker into even closer contact with the Santa Rosa Wilderness. This is a continuation hike from Horsethief Creek, traveling an additional 2 miles to a spring that, unfortunately, is often dry. Still, this trail provides some scenic vistas of Martinez Mountain and chaparral covered slopes of the vast watershed known as Horsethief Creek. If the winter rains have been abundant, then the hiker is treated to a scattering of mini-waterfalls cascading from the northern face of the Santa Rosa Mountains which form the boundary of the hiker's southern horizon.

DIRECTIONS   Follow the directions for Hike 62.

The trail continues on the eastern side of the creek with a steep climb up a sometimes slippery slope. You reach the top after climbing 400 feet and can then see the wide mountain vistas of the Horsethief Creek Basin. After hiking 0.25 mile at the top, you drop down into a delightful, small canyon that slowly winds itself ever higher and deeper into the wilderness. Sometimes a stream runs the length of this wash and helps nurture the abundant plant life.

The trail emerges from the canyon through a dense thicket of juniper and pinyon pine. It follows the wooden-post trail markers onto a level plateau. Here, the spacious views allow you to see the wilderness area, hidden from the desert dwellers below by the cover of the lower foothills. Martinez Mountain grows ever larger as you approach Cactus Spring. You will know you're there when to your left you see a dense cover of grasses flowing down into the wash. Other than that, in the dry season Cactus Spring is only a name.

The Salton Sea viewed from atop Martinez Mountain

I am especially fond of this hike because of the clean, crisp air, heavily scented with juniper and pine mixed with the aroma of the more arid desert plants. Along the final mile, the hike feels energizing and wild. The wilderness shows no sign of human presence and the sprawl of the Coachella Valley below is completely hidden from view. Weather-wise, October and March seem to be the best times to visit, with early spring offering the hiker plenty of blooming cacti and wildflowers.

64 *Agua Alta Spring*

(see map on page 126)

LENGTH: 22 miles

HIKING TIME: 11 hours

ELEVATION GAIN: 2,400 feet

DIFFICULTY: Strenuous

SEASON: October to April

INFORMATION: USDA Forest Service, Idyllwild, (909) 659-2117

The trail to Agua Alta Spring is the last part of the Cactus Spring Trail that can be hiked in a day, and it is a strenuous, long one. This segment takes the hiker into the farthest reaches of the Santa Rosa Wilderness. It conjures up images and feelings of a forgotten past, when the Cahuilla Indians roamed the canyons and slopes surrounding Martinez Mountain, gathering pinyon pine nuts and edible cacti to survive the harsh Sonoran desert lifestyle. The views in the recesses of upper Martinez Canyon are ones of desolate slopes and sheer rocky canyon walls, with the searing desert floor in the distance. It is a journey worth taking, challenging the hiker's inner spirit to make peace with the empty stillness of this unique wilderness environment.

DIRECTIONS Follow the directions for Hike 62.

You will continue from Cactus Spring, heading left into the large wash and following the wooden-post trail markers. After more than a mile, the trail turns slowly right and winds its way up toward the saddle that separates Martinez Mountain from Horsethief Creek Basin.

The trail continues down through several dry washes. Magnificent views of the surrounding canyons will awe the hiker, as well as the 6,500-foot Martinez Mountain to the left. At any rate, in the vicinity of the southern back side of this mountain, you can choose to climb to its top, but there is no trail and the rock scrambling can exhaust even the hardiest hiker. If you continue past Martinez

Mountain you will reach Agua Alta Spring at a point 6 miles from Horsethief Creek. This trail section is faint in places and requires some bushwhacking. The hike back to the trailhead is long and hot in the late spring, so I suggest you carry at least 4 quarts of water. Once the trek is finished, the hiker can seek refreshments at the Sugarloaf Cafe.

The Desert Divide and the San Jacinto Mountains

65 Santa Rosa Mountain Road to Toro Peak

LENGTH: 3 miles

HIKING TIME: 2 hours

ELEVATION GAIN: 800 feet

DIFFICULTY: Easy

SEASON: May to November

INFORMATION: USDA Forest Service, Idyllwild, (909) 659-2117

The climb to Toro Peak is a short 800-foot elevation gain, but with a spectacular vista payoff. At 8,716 feet, Toro Peak dominates the Santa Rosa Mountain Range. The stunning views from the top encompass the entire east-to-west Santa Rosa Mountains, the Coachella Valley and Salton Sea, the San Jacinto Mountains, and the sprawling Anza-Borrego State Park and deserts reaching all the way to Mexico. Toro Peak, however, is no longer the wilderness destination it once was. The Marine Corps laid claim to the peak by building a radio-relay/TV microwave station on the summit.

DIRECTIONS

To reach the trailhead, drive south on Hwy. 74 from Palm Desert and Hwy. 111, going 20 miles to the Santa Rosa Mountain Road. This is a "dirt road," suitable for 4WD vehicles, and after a rough winter can be brutal, with large potholes and eroded gullies. After driving almost 12 miles you will encounter a locked gate. Park where convenient, being careful not to block other traffic.

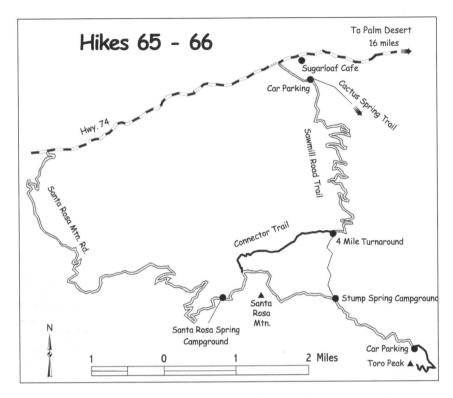

The trail is actually the road past the locked gate, and continues up for almost 1.25 miles. At the road fork, turn right and climb the very steep remaining roadway to the summit.

The vistas are outstanding, giving you a good feel for this peak as a true "island in the sky." You can explore the summit area, bushwhack to any interesting nearby destinations, and eventually backtrack to your vehicle.

Toro Peak in winter

66 *Sawmill Road Trail/Toro Peak*

LENGTH: 10 – 18 miles

HIKING TIME: 4 – 8 hours

ELEVATION GAIN: 2,500 – 4,500 ft

DIFFICULTY: Strenuous

SEASON: March to November

INFORMATION: USDA Forest Service, Idyllwild, (909) 659-2117

The Sawmill Road Trail currently provides the only access up the north-facing slope of Toro Peak and the Santa Rosa Mountains. Hikers enjoy spectacular views by looking west toward the San Jacinto Mountains, northeast down Deep Canyon, and east toward Martinez Mountain.

San Jacinto and San Gorgonio peaks, the latter being the highest point in Southern California

DIRECTIONS
To reach the trailhead, follow the directions in Hike 62 for Horsethief Creek Trail. After parking and heading east down the dirt trail, the hiker connects to a larger dirt road heading up the mountain. This is Sawmill Road Trail.

The trail winds relentlessly up the mountain. As it does, it gives the hiker magnificent views of the Coachella Valley and perhaps the only good view of the impressive Deep Canyon that borders Hwy. 74 to the east all the way up to

Sugarloaf Cafe. Sawmill Road presents a quick ascent into the cooler pine forests near Santa Rosa Peak, provides a great exercise/cardiovascular workout, and allows hikers a route up to the "twin peaks" of Toro and Santa Rosa.

After almost 5 miles straight up, you will arrive at the treeline and encounter the stone remains of a kilnlike structure. At this point hikers can turn around, having done a good 10-mile round-trip jaunt. A more strenuous hike continues just right and beyond the kiln and picks up the newly constructed "connector trail," which will take you to the top of the mountain, connecting you to the Santa Rosa Road after a 2-plus mile hike. From there turn left and continue toward the end of the trail, where the trail finishes sharply up at the top of Toro Peak and a mass of radio towers surrounding the peak. Spectacular views of the Salton Sea Basin and Anza-Borrego Desert to the south are the rewards for this very demanding hike.

Should you for some reason fail to find the connector trail, hike ⅛ mile farther past the kiln and bear left until you see an old sign indicating a trail up to the top of Santa Rosa Road. Upon connecting to the road, turn left and continue several miles until reaching the Toro Peak area.

67 Palm Canyon Pines-to-Palms Trail

LENGTH: 16 miles

HIKING TIME: 8 hours

ELEVATION LOSS: 3,200 feet

DIFFICULTY: Strenuous

SEASON: October to April

INFORMATION: USDA Forest Service, Idyllwild, (909) 659-2117

This is a five-star hike, a must for serious hikers wanting to visit, in one day, flora and fauna ranging from Canadian-type pine to Mexico's Sonoran deserts. The time of year is critical for doing this hike. It may start out cool if not cold at the top (4,000 feet), but end in blistering heat of 90-plus degrees in the lower reaches of Palm Canyon's desert area (800 feet). This hike is also best taken with hikers who have done the trail before, and should not be attempted alone. This is because the trail follows much of Palm Canyon's sandy bottom, exits at places easy to miss, and can be washed out or seriously eroded if the winter rains have been heavy. In 1994 a fire ravaged the entire area, burning almost 5 miles of this 16-mile hike. This further eroded what was once a well-maintained trail used by both hikers and mountain bikers.

DIRECTIONS

To reach the trailhead, turn south onto Hwy. 74 from Hwy. 111 in Palm Desert. After 18 miles you will reach the Ribbonwood area. Turn to your right at Pine View Drive and proceed to its end, 0.1 mile from the highway. At the time of printing this book, the Forest Service is planning another trailhead that will originate in the Pinyon Flats Campground. Check with them for changed trailhead directions.

After parking, begin hiking down the road and veer right when you see the small sign indicating the riding trail. Even if you miss this, the trail is an obvious downgrade along the ridge of the mountain. For the next several miles you will encounter mesquite, sage, yucca, and pinyon and juniper pines. The views are fantastic, looking north, west, and east. A "valley" of mountains sprawls before you in all directions and you get a clear overview of the Palm Canyon watershed plunging into the long, deepening form of the canyon itself.

After 3 miles, you will drop down into Palm Canyon from the ridge. Along the way you will see a sign indicating a ridge route. Take this ridge route to avoid dropping into the canyon too early. Once in the canyon, follow the wash to the left where it joins up with the main canyon. A quick climb over a small hill will reveal a beautiful stand of cottonwood, often brilliant yellow in early November.

When you reach the main body of Palm Canyon, turn right and follow the combination wash and trail. Always stay on the right side of the canyon. Over the next several miles you will do many 10- to 20-foot climbs above the canyon. This trail continues through washes and up the canyon side for several more miles until you reach the sign indicating Live Oak Spring. The trail then con-tinues up the right side of the canyon. You can measure your distance easily enough by noting the mileage markers that tell how far you are from Hwy. 74. After the marker says 6 miles, and you continue for another 2 miles or so, look for the mountains to the west to begin forming some steep drops into Palm Canyon. In this sec-tion of the hike, the canyon narrows and deepens. Water in late winter

Canyon Gorge along the Pines-to-Palms Trail

rushes through the rocky gorges, and several waterfalls grace the slopes above the canyon. This area is known as Upper Paradise and makes a good lunch stop. Trees and pools of water are abundant, with the first fan palms now beginning to appear. From this point, the Indian Trading Post in Palm Canyon (the northern end of this spectacular hike) is only three hours away.

As the trail continues toward Palm Springs, the San Jacinto Mountains increase in size and dominate the western view. You are literally hiking through a valley of mountains. The trail connects with a wash that takes you several miles until you see another rock duck to your right. You will know you are at this junction because the trail drops down from the right and continues across the wash and to the left. Take the trail up the right side of the hill and continue the last several miles until you finally drop down into the thick grove of Washingtonian palms that gives Palm Canyon its name. You are now just a mile from the trading post. Wind your way to the left while staying to the right of the stream. The trail

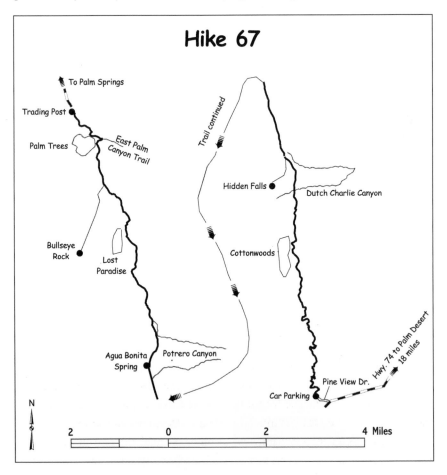

Hike 67

follows the stream, veers right, and passes a large side canyon on your left. Stay right, cross the stream where it's safe, and follow the trail to the trading post.

You have just finished an all-day adventure that, for many, opens up the natural wonders and beauty of this desert playground like nothing else can ever do. I suggest that any hiker unfamiliar with the trail contact the Coachella Valley Hiking Club at (760) 345-6234. This hiking group does the Pines-to-Palms Trail twice a year and will gladly furnish you with any information you need. To make this hike in one day, have someone drop you off at the upper trailhead on Hwy. 74 and pick you up at the trading post in Palm Canyon (also known as Hermit's Bench). If you are a strong hiker and begin hiking at 7 a.m., you will reach the Indian Trading Post no later than 3 to 4 p.m.

68 South Fork of the Pacific Crest Trail

LENGTH: 11 miles

HIKING TIME: 6 hours

ELEVATION GAIN: 800 feet

DIFFICULTY: Strenuous

SEASON: September to May

INFORMATION: USDA Forest Service, Idyllwild, (909) 659-2117

The Pacific Crest Trail (PCT) is the western answer to the eastern Appalachian Trail. Each runs south to north along the predominant mountain ranges found inland from both oceans. Both are over 2,000 miles in length. The PCT crosses near the Coachella Valley at the junction of Hwy. 74 and Hwy. 371 in Garner Valley. The trail reaches out and climbs to the ridge above the desert known as the Desert Divide, proceeds west along the ridge to the mountains above Idyllwild, and drops down the northwest side of San Jacinto Mountain into Banning Pass, crossing over I-10 before heading north toward the Big Bear/Lake Arrowhead area. The South Fork is that section heading south toward Mexico, where the PCT meets Hwy. 74. It is a world apart from the North Fork, which is just across the highway and not nearly as warm and desertlike as its southern counterpart.

The trail first takes you through sage and low brush, up a mountainside and along a low ridge. From here you can see the mountainous terrain that makes up the northern PCT route, and the magnificent vista of San Jacinto Mountain. The trail swings alongside the mountain for 2 miles. To the left you will eventually see a steep canyon network that marks the northern watershed for the Anza-Borrego Desert, 20 miles to the southeast. You will also glimpse row after row

DIRECTIONS

To reach the trailhead for both the South and North Forks, take Hwy. 74 out of Palm Desert (south at the Hwy. 111 junction) and proceed 23 miles. Or, from Hemet, drive 0.5 mile east of the Hwy. 371 junction. There is a PCT sign on the right indicating a parking area. Park and cross the highway to the south, where you will come to a gate that opens onto the trail. The sign here indicates mileage south of this point. The South Fork described here goes 0.75 mile beyond Table Mountain Road.

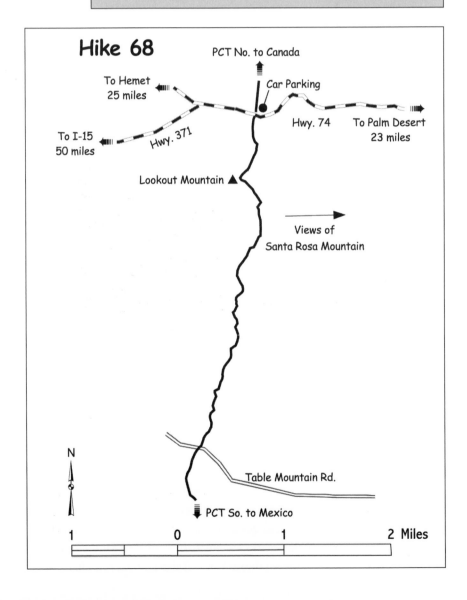

Hike 68

PCT No. to Canada

To Hemet
25 miles

Car Parking

To I-15
50 miles

Hwy. 371

Hwy. 74   To Palm Desert
23 miles

Lookout Mountain ▲

Views of
Santa Rosa Mountain

N

Table Mountain Rd.

PCT So. to Mexico

1   0   1   2 Miles

of distant mountain ranges, while to the right rise low hills whose deep green winter color suggests a hike in Wales. Passing through a flat meadow area, the trail begins a series of down-and-up wash crossings and alternating hill climbs. To the east this hike shows you the best view of Santa Rosa Mountain's southwestern flank.

After 4.5 miles the PCT reaches Table Mountain Road. Continue on for another 0.75 mile for a great view of Anza Valley. More important, in late March and early April the trail turn-around point is a field of brilliant golden California poppies that can serve as a colorful and restful lunch stop. Please note the weather conditions, as this trail can get very hot (100 degrees) in September or April if no Pacific onshore winds are blowing.

San Jacinto Mountains as viewed from the South Fork

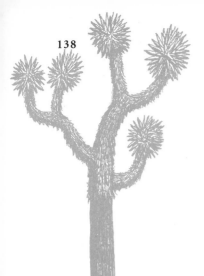

Joshua Tree National Park
Hikes 69 – 77

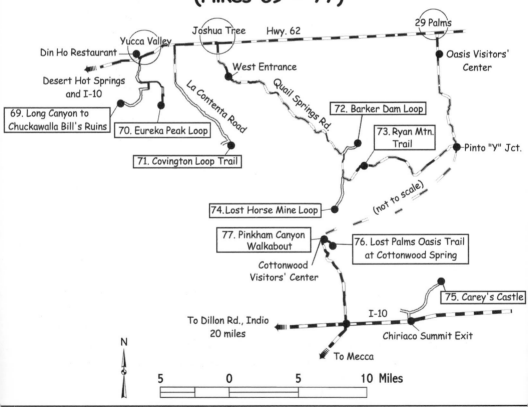

Trailhead Locations in Joshua Tree National Park (Hikes 69 - 77)

Joshua Tree   Hwy. 62

29 Palms

Yucca Valley

Din Ho Restaurant

Oasis Visitors' Center

West Entrance

Desert Hot Springs and I-10

La Contenta Road

Quail Springs Rd.

69. Long Canyon to Chuckawalla Bill's Ruins

72. Barker Dam Loop

70. Eureka Peak Loop

73. Ryan Mtn. Trail

Pinto "Y" Jct.

71. Covington Loop Trail

(not to scale)

74. Lost Horse Mine Loop

77. Pinkham Canyon Walkabout

76. Lost Palms Oasis Trail at Cottonwood Spring

Cottonwood Visitors' Center

75. Carey's Castle

To Dillon Rd., Indio 20 miles

I-10

Chiriaco Summit Exit

N

To Mecca

5   0   5   10 Miles

69 Long Canyon to Chuckawalla Bill's Ruins

LENGTH: 12 miles

HIKING TIME: 6 hours

ELEVATION GAIN: 1,800 feet

DIFFICULTY: Strenuous

SEASON: October to May

INFORMATION: Joshua Tree National Park, Twentynine Palms, (760) 367-5500

This hike takes you from the Joshua Tree National Park area through interesting, scenic Long Canyon and finally to the remains of prospector Chuckawalla Bill's roofless stone cabin. The hike through the wash can be quite tiring wherever you reach sand, although much of this trail is on hard wash bottom, so be sure to carry enough cool water and food.

DIRECTIONS

To begin this hike, drive west on I-10 to Hwy. 62, turn and travel north until you reach Yucca Valley. There, turn right on Joshua Lane, right at Warren Vista, and drive until you reach the corner of Andreas Road. The pavement ends here and a 4WD vehicle is recommended (high clearance). Turn right onto the dirt road and go 0.5 mile, then left onto the next dirt road (after 1.2 miles you will see a barbed wire fence indicating the national park boundary). Proceed another 0.5 mile, turn left, and go up the road toward the radio tower. Park after 0.3 mile at a row of five metal culverts beside a stone drainage ditch.

Head south 100 yards to the trailhead, down about 0.5 mile of rocky trail, over a 15-foot rock scramble, and into the bottom of Long Canyon Wash. There are many side washes but this will not pose a problem if you mark your way with arrows and rocks for your return as you head down the main wash in a southerly direction. Continue south, down Long Canyon Wash to reach Chuckawalla Bill's Wash. The distant Santa Rosa Mountains, to the south, will assist you in finding your way. You will eventually pass through a slick rock chute where the Santa Rosa Mountains shortly become visible before disappearing, then reappearing at the point where the wash widens. Here, vehicle tracks are often seen, and the Joshua trees thin out dramatically. After you have hiked 1.5 miles from the rock chute, on the left side is a 2-foot rock cairn and on the right side the earth has washed away from the hillside, exposing rusty brown soil and rocks. This wash heads west to take you to Chuckawalla Bill's cabin.

You will find scattered metal and wood pieces in the wash as you walk up to the roofless stone cabin. There is a spring about 100 yards past the cabin, which is visible after a wet spell.

This is an interesting "wilderness"-type hike, but first-time hikers might think of going with someone familiar with the trail and all its intricacies.

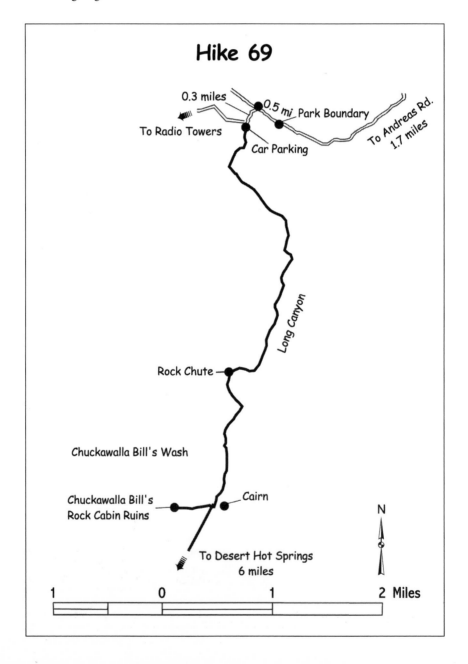

Hike 69

0.3 miles

0.5 mi. Park Boundary

To Radio Towers

Car Parking

To Andreas Rd. 1.7 miles

Long Canyon

Rock Chute

Chuckawalla Bill's Wash

Chuckawalla Bill's Rock Cabin Ruins

Cairn

To Desert Hot Springs 6 miles

N

1   0   1   2 Miles

70 *Eureka Peak Loop*

LENGTH: 10 miles

HIKING TIME: 6 hours

ELEVATION GAIN: 1,500 feet

DIFFICULTY: Strenuous

SEASON: September to May

INFORMATION: Joshua Tree National Park, Twentynine Palms, (760) 367-5500

Eureka Peak, at 5,518 feet, commands a dominating view of the western boundary of Joshua Tree National Park, including the lower Coachella Valley, San Jacinto Mountain, and San Gorgonio Peak. For this reason it is well worth the effort of struggling up sandy washes and over steep ridges to gain the heights and subsequent views afforded by Eureka Peak. The hike itself offers the flora of high desert (4,000 to 5,000 feet) in a myriad of small canyons and washes leading up to the peak. In spring the hiker is treated to cooler temperatures compared to the searing heat below, and the vegetation after a wet winter is abundantly green.

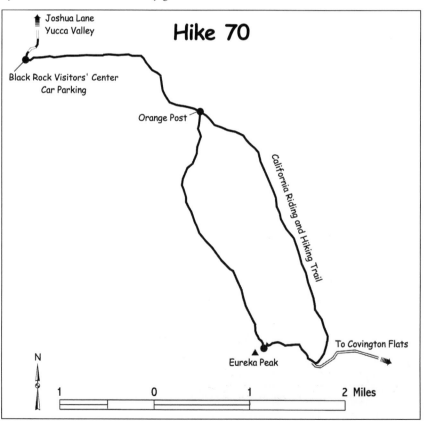

DIRECTIONS
Begin this hike by driving from I-10 to Hwy. 62, north into Yucca Valley. Just past Yucca Valley take the road to the right, Joshua Lane, at the junction with Hwy. 247, and continue into Black Rock Canyon Visitor's Center. The trail begins north of the visitor's center, east of the parking area.

The trail sign at this point indicates the California Riding and Hiking Trail, marked by brown posts. Stay on this trail for 2 miles until the trail enters a large wash and forks. Take the right fork (south) marked by an orange post. In about 0.5 mile the wash forks again. Take the small wash right, to where it ends at a small gully. Another orange marking post will direct you to the left for a climb over a ridge. From here, head to the south side of Eureka Peak, almost 5 miles from your starting point. Even if the trail appears poorly marked, tracks from previous hikers will help you find your way.

To return, after you've taken in the wonderful views from the top, head east and down perhaps 0.5 mile until you reach the junction with the California Riding and Hiking Trail. Turn left and follow this trail all the way back to your starting point. The route is mainly flat and down, through a series of washes and small valleys. It's a good idea to inquire at the visitor's center before you start the day's hike as to the condition of the trail and any improvements made in marking it.

71 *Covington Loop Trail*

LENGTH: 6 miles

HIKING TIME: 4 hours

ELEVATION GAIN: 400 feet

DIFFICULTY: Moderate

SEASON: October to June

INFORMATION: Joshua Tree National Park, Twentynine Palms, (760) 367-5500

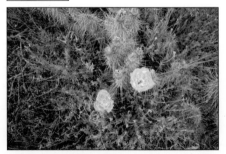

Prickly pear cactus in bloom

The Covington Loop Trail is an easy but scenic introduction to the back-country of Joshua Tree National Park. This hike makes a loop through Lower and Upper Covington Flats, past some of the largest Joshua trees in the park, with a good offering of high-desert vegetation, including juniper, yucca, and pinyon pine.

DIRECTIONS

From Palm Springs drive west on I-10 until you reach Hwy. 62. Turn right (north) toward Joshua Tree National Park and drive about 25 miles to Yucca Valley and La Contenta Road. Turn right at La Contenta Road, going to road's end at Yucca Trail and La Contenta Road. Continue across Yucca Trail to the dirt road in front of you and proceed 1.75 miles to the Covington Flat Area sign. Here turn left and drive another 5-plus miles until you reach a sign that indicates a picnic area to the left. Take this road left for another mile or so and park near the picnic tables (a distance of 6.5 miles from the first Covington Flat Area sign).

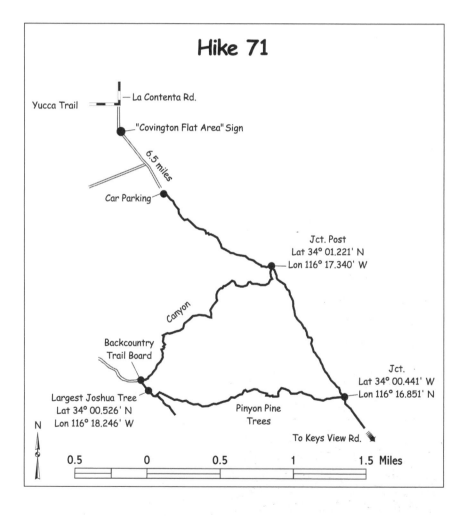

Hike 71

Yucca Trail — La Contenta Rd.

"Covington Flat Area" Sign

6.5 miles

Car Parking

Jct. Post
Lat 34° 01.221' N
Lon 116° 17.340' W

Canyon

Backcountry
Trail Board

Jct.
Lat 34° 00.441' W
Lon 116° 16.851' N

Largest Joshua Tree
Lat 34° 00.526' N
Lon 116° 18.246' W

Pinyon Pine
Trees

To Keys View Rd.

N

0.5   0   0.5   1   1.5 Miles

The trail starts in back of the trail sign just east of the parking area. Head down this trail southeast through a rather extensive burn area. The trail will cross into a wash and rise onto a plateau, but is marked by signposts along the way. After 2 miles you will reach another metal sign indicating Keys View Road and Covington Flats. Turn right in a northeasterly direction and soon you will be climbing out of the burn area and up into a green, high-desert hill region covered in pinyon pine. Enjoy the cooler green plateau that sharply contrasts with the burn area you just left.

After almost 2 miles you will reach another parking area with a backcountry map/register sign. Just in back of the sign a small path makes its way down and into a larger wash. Head northeast (left) into the large canyon in front of you. As you enter the canyon keep to the right. You will be forced to bushwhack through overgrown vegetation and scramble down many small, dry, rock waterfall formations. Even when the route appears impassable, keep to the right and carefully slide down the rock formations to pick up the canyon trail along the canyon bottom. This canyon is fun to negotiate and contrasts with the flat sections of the hike. After 1.5 miles the canyon will lead you back into the open area you first hiked through. As the canyon empties into the wash, bear left and eventually you will meet the signposts you passed as you first negotiated the wash. Once you're at this juncture, turn left along the trail and head back to the parking lot where you first came from. Spring (March-May) should reward the hiker with flowers in the canyon and wash areas, provided enough rain has fallen.

72 *Barker Dam Loop*

LENGTH: 1 mile

HIKING TIME: 2 hours

ELEVATION GAIN: 0 feet

DIFFICULTY: Easy

SEASON: October to June

INFORMATION: Joshua Tree National Park, Twentynine Palms, (760) 367-5500

Joshua Tree National Park is a maze of huge boulders, uplifted mountains, and exotic high-mountain desert plants. One of the key areas in the park for viewing the sometimes strange and unique rock formations is the Wonderland of Rocks, where a man-made dam has captured water and runoff and created a small but unique lake. The area boasts interesting boulder formations, and the hike, while short, makes a good diversion from the more strenuous hikes the park has to offer.

DIRECTIONS To reach the Wonderland of Rocks area, take Hwy. 62 off I-10, north to Joshua Tree. Continue through town until you come to the turnoff to the right for the park entrance. Once at the fee station, drive another 10 miles to the Hidden Valley Campground, where a dirt road leads you another 2 miles to the Barker Dam parking area.

From north of the parking area, take the signed interpretive trail, highlighting the local desert plant life, into the Wonderland of Rocks. The trail leads into the Barker Dam area, where it meanders along the lake. From here you can explore whatever strikes your interest before returning.

Three million years ago, volcanic eruptions left behind a few nongranitic rocks in the park, like those seen at Malapai Hill, a 400-foot-high hill of black basalt

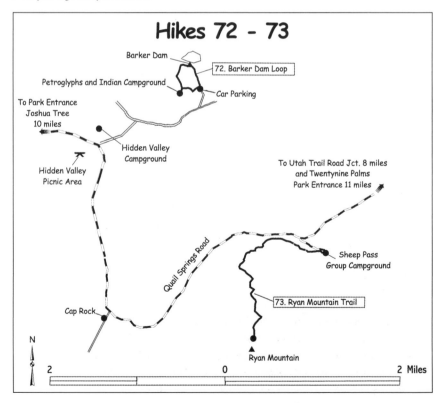

Hikes 72 - 73

Barker Dam

| 72. Barker Dam Loop |

Petroglyphs and Indian Campground

Car Parking

To Park Entrance
Joshua Tree
10 miles

Hidden Valley
Campground

Hidden Valley
Picnic Area

To Utah Trail Road Jct. 8 miles
and Twentynine Palms
Park Entrance 11 miles

Quail Springs Road

Sheep Pass
Group Campground

| 73. Ryan Mountain Trail |

Cap Rock

N

Ryan Mountain

2   0   2 Miles

73 *Ryan Mountain Trail*
(see map on page 145)

LENGTH: 4 miles

HIKING TIME: 3 hours

ELEVATION GAIN: 700 feet

DIFFICULTY: Moderate

SEASON: October to May

INFORMATION: Joshua Tree National Park, Twentynine Palms, (760) 367-5500

The top of Ryan Mountain offers one of the best circular views of the surrounding scenic features found in Joshua Tree National Park. The views include the high summits of San Jacinto Peak and San Gorgonio Peak, Pinto Basin, Lost Horse Valley, the Wonderland of Rocks, and the Little San Bernardino Mountains, forming the northern border of the Coachella Valley. The well-maintained trail is considered a moderate hike, but if taken at a slow pace, can be done as an easy hike.

DIRECTIONS

To begin, drive south 3 miles on Utah Trail Road from the Joshua Tree National Park Visitors Center at Twentynine Palms. Stay right at the Pinto "Y" junction and drive 8.5 miles until you reach the Ryan Mountain Trailhead parking lot on your left. Do not park at Sheep Pass Campground as this is reserved for campers.

Hikers are rewarded with a beautiful view of Pleasant Valley

74 *Lost Horse Mine Loop*

LENGTH: 8 miles

HIKING TIME: 4 hours

ELEVATION GAIN: 600 feet

DIFFICULTY: Moderate

SEASON: September to June

INFORMATION: Joshua Tree National Park, Twentynine Palms, (760) 367-5500

Located near the center of Joshua Tree National Park, the Lost Horse Mine Loop Trail combines three hikes into one—offering hikers a visit to a once-successful working gold mine, some of the most spectacular desert-mountain vistas in Southern California, and a delightful meander through a gentle wash filled with Joshua trees, yucca, juniper, and many other high-desert plants. Add to these the views looking south toward the Coachella Valley and you have the makings of a really fine day hike that introduces you to the stunning natural beauty of Joshua Tree National Park.

DIRECTIONS
To begin this hiking adventure, drive north on Hwy. 62, off I-10, just a few miles west of Palm Springs. Continue north into the town of Joshua Tree, where you will turn right at the sign indicating the Joshua Tree National Park entrance (Park Boulevard). Continue through a sparse scattering of homes until you reach the park entrance. After paying the fee, continue through the park to Cap Rock Junction, where you will turn right onto Keys View Road and drive for another 2.5 miles. On the left, look for the dirt road directing you to Lost Horse Mine.

After parking, begin hiking the trail found east of the parking lot and starting just past the interpretive display. The trail takes you up for 2 miles until reaching your first destination, the Lost Horse Mine. Here you can explore the remains of this mine and read about its history. Continue on the same trail you came in on, but be aware that from this point on there will be few hikers, as most choose to reach the mine and return to their vehicles before pushing on to another destination in the park.

Less than 0.5 mile from the mine, the trail climbs to a series of fantastic overlooks into Lost Horse, Queen, and Pleasant valleys, and even to the distant, jagged Coxcomb Mountains, marking the farthest eastern boundary of the park.

The trail begins a descent along a ridge and gives you a good feel for the rugged desert mountain environment. In less than a mile you will come to a large hole that marks a previously used mine shaft. Continue hiking, noting a series of rock cairns along the right side of the trail. From the large hole, travel about 0.25 mile until you see both a rock cairn to your right and a low saddle about 100 feet above you. Leave the trail at this point, rock scrambling up the slope to the top. From there, head south by southwest down, sometimes over low ridges, until you see the remains of a tall, stone fireplace 40 to 100 yards below. Hike down to this area and explore what's left of a prospector's once proud home. The trail picks up just west of the fireplace, and the distance from where you left the main trail is no more than 0.5 mile. If finding this part of the Lost Horse Mine Loop Trail proves too difficult, backtrack to the main trail and return to your vehicle by hiking past the mine and down the mountain.

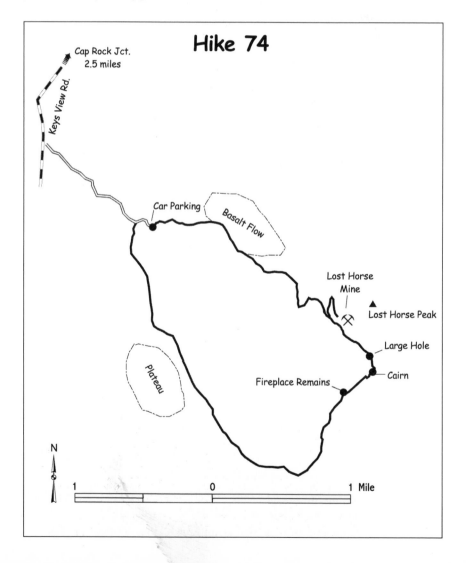

If you are successful in connecting with the loop via the fireplace remains, continue on the trail, climbing to a wonderful plateau offering great views of the Santa Rosa Mountains and San Jacinto Peak. In another mile, after you've exited a short, dry wash, you will reach a turn to the right, marked by rock cairns. For the next 1.5 miles you will be hiking through a flat but delightful valley, making your way over sandy trails marked sporadically by cairns. This section of trail takes you directly back to the parking lot. You will find that the

trail bears right at any junction and keeps you in a desert wash bordered on both sides by low mountains.

The Lost Horse Mine is the best preserved old mining operation in the park

75 *Carey's Castle*

LENGTH: 8 miles

HIKING TIME: 5 hours

ELEVATION GAIN: 1,400 feet

DIFFICULTY: Strenuous

SEASON: October to May

INFORMATION: Joshua Tree National Park, Cottonwood Spring Visitor's Center (760) 367-5500

DIRECTIONS

The adventure begins by driving on I-10 for almost 26 miles east of the Dillon Road exit in Indio. Take the Chiriaco Summit exit, turning left toward the General Patton Museum. Drive on the dirt road found between the museum and the coffee shop (the sign reads "RV Parking") for 0.5 mile until you reach the aqueduct road at the large "T" intersection. Turn onto this road, driving almost 3.5 miles. To your left, look for a rock cairn marking a small parking area.

Joshua Tree National Park is the home to many abandoned mines and ruins of former prospectors. None compare, however, to "Carey's Castle." Sometime around 1940, a prospector by the name of Carey dug a mine shaft in the southern, desolate, rugged low mountains bordering Joshua Tree. He built his home (castle) under a huge boulder, as a single-room shelter, and finished the front with stonework, framing a small wooden doorway. His mine is located just 0.25 mile west of the castle. The hike up to this ruin is adventurous, as you must negotiate a series of beautiful canyons and dry falls, with plenty of big boulder hopping and scrambling. This hike is best taken with someone who knows the way, as no real trail exists to the "castle."

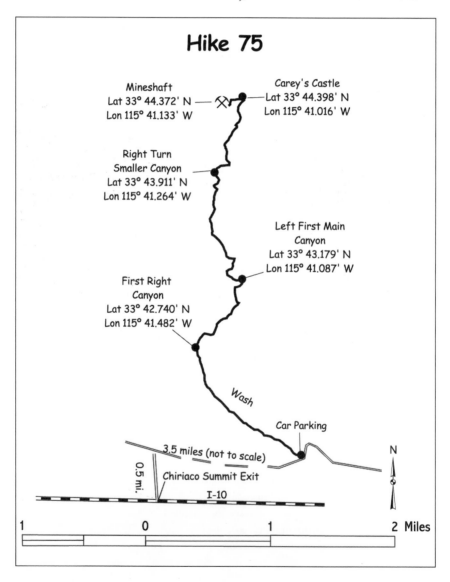

Head north up the desert wash, through beautiful blooming flowers, cacti, and ocotillo in March and April.

After 1 mile take a right at the first large canyon. Hike up this canyon until reaching the first main canyon where you turn left, then left again where it is next possible. This section lasts about 1 to 1.5 miles and includes a lot of boulder scrambling. The canyon eventually reaches another main branch. Here, take the smaller canyon to the right. You will gradually climb out of the canyon and onto the plateau area of Carey's Castle, the shelter built beneath the large boulder found to the right of the canyon's end. Head west on the dirt trail for about 0.25 mile to see the remains of the mine shaft. Both the views and the feeling of the place are rugged, wild, and captivating. Boulder-flanked mountains dominate the landscape and invite further exploring.

Known for massive rock outcroppings like Jumbo Rocks (pictured), Joshua Tree National Park attracts climbers from all over the country

76 *Lost Palms Oasis Trail at Cottonwood Spring*

LENGTH: 8 miles

HIKING TIME: 4 hours

ELEVATION GAIN: 400 feet

DIFFICULTY: Moderate

SEASON: September to May

INFORMATION: Joshua Tree National Park, Twentynine Palms, (760) 367-5500

On the southernmost boundary of Joshua Tree National Park, several minor earthquake fault lines, branches of the San Andreas fault line 20 miles southwest, cut through the low mountains overlooking I-10. By doing so, the fault encourages water to seep to the surface. At one such point a large, lush growth of California fan palms can be explored and admired for their stately beauty. This particular grouping of fan palms has come to be known as Lost Palms Oasis, and makes a beautiful day hike through washes and over plateaus, offering stunning views of the surrounding mountains and valleys, including the distant San Jacinto Mountains to the west.

DIRECTIONS

To reach the Lost Palms Oasis Trailhead, travel almost 20 miles past Indio, heading east on I-10. Exit at the Joshua Tree National Park off ramp, turn left on the road leading into the park, and drive the 8 miles to Cottonwood Spring Visitor's Center. There you will find additional material about the national park as well as a campground.

The best time for this hike is early spring (February to April) or October to November. It can get hot in the afternoon during those renowned warm times of year for this desert region, so carry an ample supply of cool water.

The trail begins east of the visitor's center. You head immediately up a gradual rising slope, then pass through a series of washes. Look for the

Formerly a National Monument, Joshua Tree was promoted to National Park status in 1994, and was extended by 230,000 acres—mainly remote mountainous regions

brown trail markers as you pass through the sandy washes. In springtime the flowers and astonishingly rich plant life will entice you to stop and enjoy the flora. As you climb, look to your rear for beautiful views of the valley and mountains surrounding this part of the park.

The trail takes you to a plateau, found at the 3-mile marker. Gaze due south for stunning vistas of the Salton Sea Basin . . . almost primeval in its rugged wilderness look. You will soon come to several small washes, out of which you'll climb until finally reaching the overlook for Lost Palms Oasis.

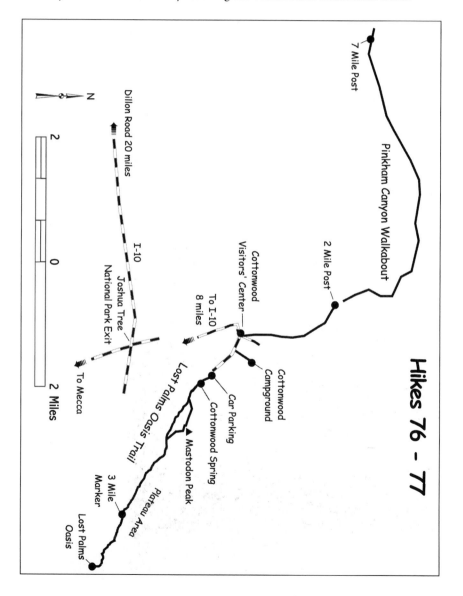

You can explore the oasis by dropping down the indicated trail, or you can just admire the beauty of both the palms and the magnificent mountains to the east. The hike on the Lost Palms Oasis Trail is more relaxing than many others because it has little elevation gain—it feels more like a walk through a nature park and gives you an intimate feel for the mixture of rugged mountains and flowering desert found especially along this trail.

77 Pinkham Canyon Walkabout

(see map on page 153)

LENGTH: 14 miles

HIKING TIME: 6 hours

ELEVATION GAIN: 100 feet

DIFFICULTY: Moderate/strenuous

SEASON: September to May

INFORMATION: Joshua Tree National Park, Twentynine Palms, (760) 367-5500

This hike should be done in the early morning to take advantage of the lighting on the colorful rock formations seen off in the distance and to the right of the trail. This "trail" is actually a jeep road that crosses a flat space of land and continues more than 14 miles west from the visitor's center into the Pinkham Canyon area.

Little San Bernardino Mountains along Pinkham Canyon

DIRECTIONS

From the Dillon Road exit off I-10, drive 21 miles east on I-10 to the Joshua Tree National Park turnoff. Turn left at the stop sign, and drive north 8 miles until you reach the Cottonwood Spring Visitor's Center. Park there and walk across the street to the dirt road located just west of the visitor's center.

The hike first heads north, then west. In back of you to the east, Eagle Mountain—at 5,350 feet—dominates the horizon.

I find this hike good for "getting away from it all," feeling free in the wide-open spaces, and, when gripped by curiosity, bushwhacking up to the nearby hills for views of the surrounding areas. Although no spectacular canyon experience awaits you at trail's end, the flat length of this hike permits an all-day nondemanding outdoor exercise experience.

You can turn back at any time to make the hike shorter without losing some of the benefits of being outside, or you can go more than 20 miles round-trip into the backcountry before calling it a day. Spring and late fall when skies are blue are the best times for this hike.

San Gorgonio Pass and Nearby

Hikes 78 – 89

Trailhead Locations in San Gorgonio Pass and Nearby (Hikes 78 - 89)

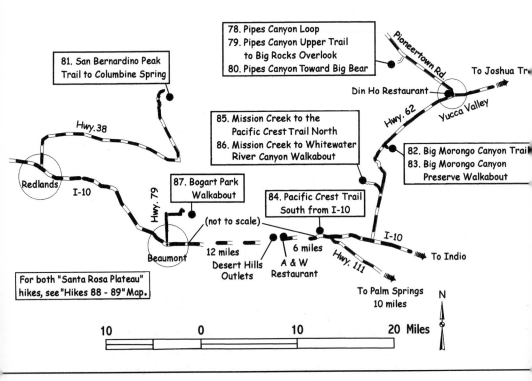

78. Pipes Canyon Loop
79. Pipes Canyon Upper Trail to Big Rocks Overlook
80. Pipes Canyon Toward Big Bear

81. San Bernardino Peak Trail to Columbine Spring

Din Ho Restaurant

Pioneertown Rd.

To Joshua Tr

Hwy. 62

Yucca Valley

Hwy. 38

85. Mission Creek to the Pacific Crest Trail North
86. Mission Creek to Whitewater River Canyon Walkabout

82. Big Morongo Canyon Trai
83. Big Morongo Canyon Preserve Walkabout

Redlands

I-10

Hwy. 79

87. Bogart Park Walkabout

84. Pacific Crest Trail South from I-10

I-10

(not to scale)

To Indio

Beaumont

12 miles
Desert Hills Outlets

6 miles
A & W Restaurant

Hwy. 111

For both "Santa Rosa Plateau" hikes, see "Hikes 88 - 89" Map.

To Palm Springs
10 miles

N

10   0   10   20 Miles

78 *Pipes Canyon Loop*

LENGTH: 7 miles

HIKING TIME: 4 hours

ELEVATION GAIN: 900 feet

DIFFICULTY: Moderate

SEASON: September to May

INFORMATION: Wildlands Conservancy, (909) 797-8507

Pipes Canyon is a conservation area of over 15,000 acres, a project of the Wildlands Conservancy. Located at 4,450 feet, this canyon/mountainous area supports a riparian woodland in the canyon, nourished by a flowing stream from the surrounding mountain snowmelt runoff. Pinyon pine, Joshua trees, goldenbush, Mojave yucca, and a generous offering of other plant species combine with bighorn sheep, mule deer, rabbits, coyote, and other animals to present the hiker with a dynamic, beautiful nature preserve accessible by three different hikes.

DIRECTIONS

From I-10, just west of Palm Springs, turn north onto Hwy. 62 toward Joshua Tree National Park. After 19 miles, in the town of Yucca Valley, turn left on Pioneertown Road. Drive 7 miles, passing Pioneertown, the old western town Hollywood set; then turn left at the Pipes Canyon Road intersection, and drive 0.6 mile; then right at the sign for Pipes Canyon, where you can park near the entry gate.

The Canyon Loop hike begins just past the entry gate. Continue walking through the canyon, sometimes crossing the stream if it's present (in a dry winter the stream can be found only after a mile of hiking), observing the variety of flora and any animals that might be about. After a mile or so you will come to a narrowing of the canyon. On your right, look for the stone house remains of an earlier settler. Soon the canyon forces you to hike in or near the water before it widens out, revealing groves of cottonwood and rushes.

As the trail enlarges, look for a desert area veering to your left. About 0.5 mile from the stone house, this desert area shows foot traffic wear. Take this side path to the first large canyon that you come to on your left. The trail then climbs steeply up the side of this canyon ravine until topping out on a saddle above the canyon. From here turn left and proceed up the hill.

For the next 1.5 miles the trail meanders up and down through undergrowth and small pinyon pine. After 0.75 mile by looking to your left and down toward the valley, you can see the three magnificent mesas you drove through: Flat Top,

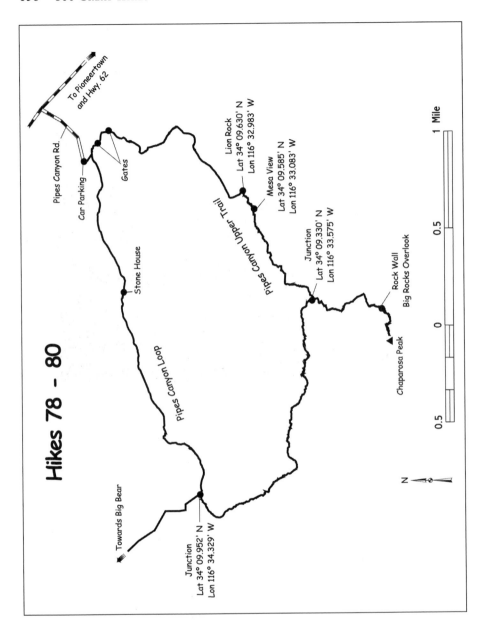

Hikes 78 - 80

Burnt Hill, and Black Hill . . . reminders of a New Mexico landscape. Near 1.5 miles from the saddle above the canyon, look for a distinct trail junction, accented by rock cairns. Take the left down turn and go 0.75 mile, noting the lava and basalt rock scattered throughout the area. This trail rises to a small hilltop before proceeding down to a major trail junction. At the junction turn left, and in 0.5 mile negotiate around a closed gate by going right. The trail then follows down a hillside before coming to the bottom, marked by two gates within yards of each other.

At the first gate go right around it, then left and uphill to the second gate, then veer left back toward the parking lot, past a large house, then down a small incline to your vehicle.

Flat Top, Burnt Hill, and Black Hill mesas are easily viewed from the Pipes Canyon Loop Trail

79 Pipes Canyon Upper Trail to Big Rocks Overlook

LENGTH: 6 miles

HIKING TIME: 3 hours

ELEVATION GAIN: 1,300 feet

DIFFICULTY: Moderate

SEASON: September to May

INFORMATION: Wildlands Conservancy, (909) 797-8507

DIRECTIONS

Follow the directions for Hike 78.

At the parking lot head up the small hill rising to the left of the fenced house, going around the gate, across a flat land area past the house on your right until you come to the dirt road that begins a downward bias. Walk through the first gate, then go left around the second gate until you get back to the jeep trail, which begins a steep climb up the mountain. Disregard "no trespassing" signs, as hikers have access rights.

At the top of the hill you will gain spectacular vistas of the nearby valleys and far mountain ranges. Look for basalt rock and other evidence of volcanic activity. You will come to a closed gate, but veer left around it to regain the trail on the other side. Continue through a pinyon pine forested area, coming around a hillside where up ahead you will see a reddish outcrop of rock. As you hike on the trail here, look to your right and down for a distinct trail marker: a lion with arrows pointing right etched on a flat stone.

Take this trail up the hillside and enjoy magnificent views of the valley below as well as Flat Top, Burnt Hill, and Black Hill mesas. The trail then proceeds down into a raised valley, offering a variety of unique rock formations to enjoy, and more lava pieces to examine. After a mile the trail meets a major junction. Turn left and continue on this trail as it winds its way through washes, up ravines, and along hillsides before topping out in a spectacular vista of what

I call the Rock Wall and Window Rock, a cut-out section of mountain that frames Toro Peak in the Santa Rosa Mountains to the distant south. Also look for Halloween Face, a unique placement of three holes in

Big Rocks Overlook offers magnificent views of the valley below

the rock wall in front of you which resembles a carved pumpkin face.

Note the small hill to your right. Bushwhack toward this hill, finding a faint trail to get you there in less than 0.5 mile. The views from the top are stunning, especially of San Jacinto Mountain with a full winter's coat of snow. Follow the trail back the same way you came to get to your vehicle.

80 *Pipes Canyon Toward Big Bear*

(see map on page 158)

LENGTH: 14-plus miles

HIKING TIME: 7 hours

ELEVATION GAIN: 2,000 feet

DIFFICULTY: Moderate/strenuous

SEASON: September to May

INFORMATION: Wildlands Conservancy, (909) 797-8507

DIRECTIONS Follow the directions for Hike 78.

After entering Pipes Canyon, hike for a mile-plus until passing the stone house, and continue through the narrow section of the canyon until the trail suddenly widens and becomes a full-fledged jeep trail. In a wet winter, the months of April and May bless this section of trail with flowering lupine, wildflowers, and greening cottonwoods. After the trail leaves the wetland area and widens, it makes a sharp right turn and begins a 20-plus mile climb toward the Big Bear mountain area. Large pinyon pines accent the trail as it climbs toward the cooler mountain heights. You will also pass a developed mountain cabin and other reminders that civilization is not too far away.

This trail is easy to follow, is gradual in its climb, and offers a great view of the higher mountain slopes ahead. Keep in mind that, though it becomes cooler as you climb, the lower portion of the canyon trail remains quite warm on a typical late spring day. This environment seems a wilderness area all your own, as foot traffic is rare and vehicle traffic almost nonexistent. Strong hikers can go a long way before turning back, enjoying a section of Southern California backroads rarely visited.

81 *San Bernardino Peak Trail to Columbine Spring*

LENGTH: 9 miles

HIKING TIME: 5 hours

ELEVATION GAIN: 2,100 feet

DIFFICULTY: Strenuous

SEASON: June to October

INFORMATION: USDA Forest Service, Mentone, (909) 794-1123

The San Gorgonio Wilderness has been described as an "Island of Wilderness in a Sea of Civilization," embracing over 59,000 acres of well-timbered slopes covered with sugar, limber, and Jeffrey pine; white fir; incense cedar; black and live oak; and a generous scattering of Douglas fir. Small meadows, lakes, and the rocky slopes of the tallest mountain in Southern California, San Gorgonio Peak (11,502 feet), highlight this area of the San Bernardino Mountains. A permit is required to hike in the wilderness and can be obtained by calling the above number.

The San Bernardino Peak Trail gives the hiker a great introduction to the many trails crisscrossing the San Bernardino Mountains, and is easily accessed from the Coachella Valley. The hike itself takes you up to 8,000 feet, affording spectacular views of the valleys below, but also shows a clear sweep of mountain ridges looking north toward Lake Arrowhead and Big Bear Lake.

DIRECTIONS

To reach the trailhead, drive to Redlands and head north on Hwy. 38. Continue to Mentone and on to the Mill Creek Ranger Station. Wilderness permits can be obtained there, but should have been called for well in advance of busy weekends. Drive 20 miles farther to the town of Angelus Oaks, turn right at the fire station, and look for the sign that indicates San Bernardino Peak Trail. Follow the dirt road to the small parking area; the trail begins at the north end of the parking lot.

The trail climbs steeply up switchbacks and through forests of pine, oak, and fir. As you ascend, the sharp rocky ridges across the valley assert themselves and dominate the horizon. After several miles, the trail begins to traverse a glorious plateau of manzanita and chaparral. From here, you can see the distant ridges of the northern San Bernardino Mountains.

The views will continue to be astounding. After almost 4.5 miles you will arrive at a side trail for Columbine Spring. You can continue down to the spring or hike farther up the trail toward Limber Pine Branch and ultimately

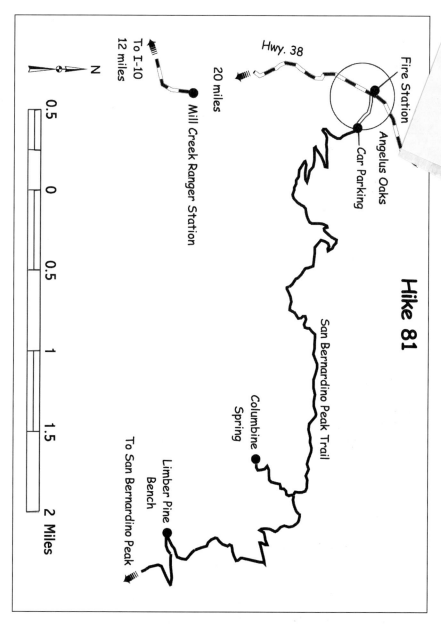

Hike 81

San Bernardino Peak (10,624 feet). The hike back down the mountain gives you the added beauty of seeing sharp mountain ridges to the west. Take a good supply of cool water during the summer, as the lower slopes near Angelus Oaks can be quite hot.

82 *Big Morongo Canyon Trail*

LENGTH: 6 miles

HIKING TIME: 4 hours

ELEVATION GAIN: 1,800 feet

DIFFICULTY: Moderate

SEASON: October to May

INFORMATION: BLM Office, Palm Springs, (760) 251-4800

Big Morongo Canyon Trail first shows hikers a lush riparian oasis—almost too rich in vegetation to be associated with the nearby desert—then plunges them through the wide, stream-fed wash of Big Morongo Canyon before bringing them to the desolate southern canyon northwest of Desert Hot Springs. This hike is best done as a shuttle from top to bottom, with an 1,800-foot elevation loss, gradually spread over a 6-mile stretch.

DIRECTIONS

The shuttle vehicles for the south end of the canyon need to drive on Hwy. 62, north from I-10, until reaching Indian Avenue. Turn right and drive for almost a mile until you come to a dirt road to the left where you will turn and park near the chain-link fence. The shuttle to the northern beginning of the trail is done by traveling up Hwy. 62 for almost 10 miles, into the town of Morongo Valley, and turning right at the sign indicating Morongo Wildlife Preserve.

High desert vegetation above Big Morongo Canyon Trail

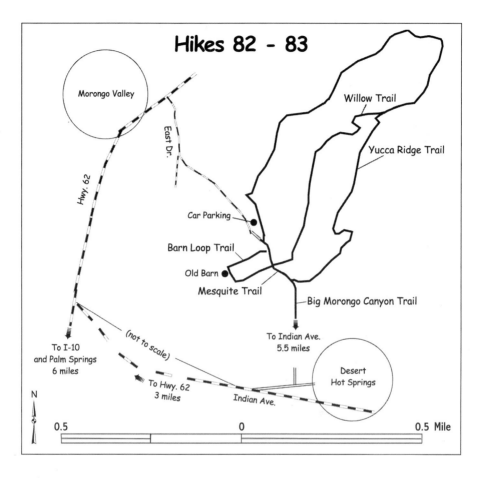

After parking, begin the trail by the interpretive displays and follow the trail/road along the creek for a mile until coming to a small dam. Up to this point the trail astounds the hiker with a look reminiscent of the Maryland wetlands, rather than the farthest reaches of the great Sonoran Desert. But this trail quickly empties you into the canyon proper, where, during the spring, you will follow a stream for almost 3 miles. Take care crossing the slippery rocks, which are often not securely anchored to the bottom. The canyon trail is really the canyon floor. Make your way as best you can, following the path of least resistance downstream past the rock- and dirt-enclosed walls of Big Morongo Canyon—where flowers are abundant in early spring—until the canyon ends 6 miles from where you began this adventure.

83 Big Morongo Canyon Preserve
Walkabout *(see map on page 165)*

LENGTH: 3 miles
HIKING TIME: 2 hours
ELEVATION GAIN: 200 feet
DIFFICULTY: Easy
SEASON: Year-round, 7:30 a.m.
to sunset

INFORMATION: BMC Preserve,
Morongo Valley, (760) 363-7190
or BLM Office, Palm Springs
(760) 251-4800

The Big Morongo Canyon area was active as a "ranch stopover" for weary travelers as far back as 1873. In recent times a partnership between The Nature Conservancy, Bureau of Land Management (BLM), and San Bernardino County Regional Parks has helped preserve and develop more than 29,000 acres for a modern-day hiking, scenic, historical, and bird-watching oasis, where lush vegetation can thrive in a riparian setting fed by mountain snowmelt.

The Big Morongo Canyon Preserve is truly seasonal. Serving as a transitional zone between the Mojave and Sonoran deserts, it offers the visitor a rich landscape suggestive of New Mexico hill country. An explosion of cottonwoods, red willows, cattails, bulrushes, and other riparian species contrasts sharply with the barren desert landscape nearby. In fall, the yellow cottonwoods scent the air with the musty odor of approaching winter, whereas in spring, vibrant, crisp shades of green reemerge to color the canyon once again.

The preserve is a favorite escape of mine—its clear, cool morning air complementing majestic San Gorgonio Peak to the west, while the mountains slope down from on high with their verdant forests. Spring is the most inviting of seasons, as more than 250 species of birds are found in the canyon. So different is this area from the nearby lower deserts that in just a few miles the visitor has traveled back both in time and in place, refreshed by the brilliant foliage and colors, odors, flowing water, and wildlife. No pets, smoking, or camping is permitted in the preserve. The area remains a true sanctuary of serene natural beauty—peaceful and refreshing to the spirit. Trail maps, birding information, and other useful materials are available on the property.

DIRECTIONS

From I-10 turn north onto Hwy. 62, just west of Palm Springs. Drive for 11.5 miles into the town of Morongo, turning right on East Drive, then left into the Big Morongo Canyon Preserve.

From the parking lot, after you read the available trail and wildlife brochures, begin discovering Big Morongo Canyon by walking east toward the trees. Five trail systems interlink, allowing for a 3-plus mile hike around the immediate canyon area. The Desert Willow Trail offers a look into nearby wetlands; the Yucca Ridge Trail climbs above the wetland and wooded areas, offering a spectacular view of the Big Morongo Canyon and San Jacinto and San Gorgonio peaks; the Barn Trail crosses grassy fields to an old barn from the 1920s ranching era; the Mesquite Trail guides you into the heart of the riparian wetlands, over boardwalks and alongside flowing streams; and the Canyon Trail takes you alongside the stream and

eventually down into the Desert Hot Springs area.

Visitors will be amazed at the year-round contrast between lush wetlands and surrounding desert slopes —and following a wet winter in March and April, those slopes support a colorful display of wild-flowers and blooming cacti. Pack a picnic lunch,

Over six miles long, the Big Morongo Canyon Preserve features 3,900 acres of virgin terrain dating back two billion years

take your camera, leave your stressful worries behind, and let the Big Morongo Canyon Preserve work its magic on you during every season of the year!

84 *Pacific Crest Trail South from I-10*

LENGTH: 10 miles

HIKING TIME: 5 hours

ELEVATION GAIN: 2,000 feet

DIFFICULTY: Strenuous

SEASON: October to May

INFORMATION: BLM Office, Palm Springs, (760) 251-4800

The Pacific Crest Trail (PCT) comes down the north face of San Jacinto Mountain, spilling over into the San Gorgonio Pass, across I-10, and northward up the slopes of the San Bernardino Mountains. The easiest access to this section of the PCT is from I-10, where you cross the flat desert before reaching the low foothills of San Jacinto Mountain and eventually the higher elevations at 9,000 feet above Snow Creek Canyon.

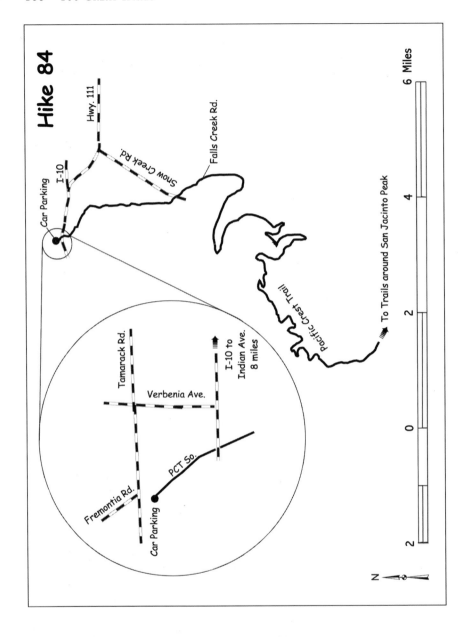

DIRECTIONS

To reach the trailhead, drive west on I-10 for 8 miles from the Indian Avenue exit. Turn north onto Verbenia Avenue, and left on Tamarack Road to Fremontia Road. The PCT starts 50 yards from the signpost, on the left side of the road.

Head south under the I-10 bridges, where you will come out into a large wash. Veer southeast toward the high-voltage lines. You may begin seeing the brown PCT trail markers, provided the spring rains have not washed them away. Head toward the second-to-last high-voltage tower from the mountainside. You will then pick up the PCT markers leading to the paved Snow Creek Road. Turn right onto Falls Creek Road to the gated lands of the Water District. Follow the paved road up 2 miles to the PCT marker on the right side of the road.

From here, the trail begins climbing the mountain, making steep switchbacks for nearly 16 miles to the top, where it connects with the trail systems around San Jacinto Peak. The views are spectacular, but unfortunately, this section of trail is too long for a casual day hike, and needs to be done as part of a two- to three-day backpack.

85 *Mission Creek to the Pacific Crest Trail North*

LENGTH: 8 miles

HIKING TIME: 5 hours

ELEVATION GAIN: 1,300 feet

DIFFICULTY: Moderate

SEASON: October to April

INFORMATION: The Wildlands Conservancy, Yucaipa (760) 369-7105

The Mission Creek Preserve is a new watershed hiking area east of San Gorgonio Mountain and west of Desert Hot Springs. This area is scheduled to open for public use by June 2000. By calling the above number, hikers can access information about this area.

DIRECTIONS

From I-10 north of Palm Springs, turn north onto Hwy. 62, going to Joshua Tree National Park. After 5 miles, and just west of Desert Hot Springs, look for the sign indicating Mission Creek Road. Turn left (west) and drive until you come to the gated access. Call for information about the operating procedures for hiking this preserve.

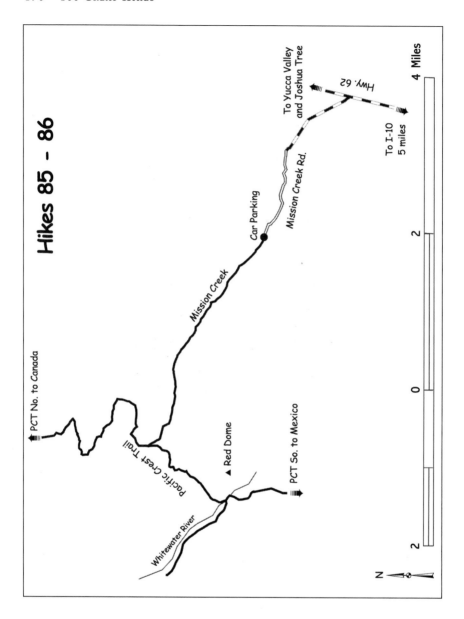

Hikes 85 – 86

The trail begins west of the houses on the preserve property, following a small streambed toward San Gorgonio Mountain. In spring, following a wet winter, this area is lush with flowers and offers great views of San Jacinto Mountain to the south. After several miles the trail connects to the Pacific Crest Trail (PCT). Turn right (north) at this trail juncture and continue winding your way along the foothills for several more miles to see beautiful ridge views from the top.

The payoff for this hike is the wildflowers found after wet winters and springs. If little rain has fallen, this trail tends to be somewhat desertlike. You can hike as far as you please on the North Fork of the PCT before turning around and hiking back to your vehicle.

San Jacinto Peak as viewed from Mission Creek

86 *Mission Creek to Whitewater River Canyon Walkabout*

LENGTH: 12 miles

HIKING TIME: 5 – 6 hours

ELEVATION GAIN: 600 feet

DIFFICULTY: Strenuous

SEASON: October to April

INFORMATION: Wildlands Conservancy, Yucaipa (760) 369-7105

DIRECTIONS
Follow the road and trail directions for Hike 85.

After reaching the PCT, turn left and wind your way along the foothills until the trail climbs up and over the low ridge overlooking the expansive Whitewater Canyon. The trail then drops down the other side and into the canyon. A jumble of large granite boulders forms the bottom of this wide canyon, where the Whitewater River flows down from San Gorgonio Mountain. The "trail" is still recognizable for some distance as it makes its way across the canyon floor. The actual route will change depending on the flood runoff from the surrounding San Gorgonio Mountains.

Pick the easiest and safest route that will eventually follow west/northwest along the Whitewater River. Boulder jumping, avoiding side streams, observing the lay of the land in front of you—these are necessary skills on this walkabout! In wet winters you will negotiate trees and other debris, uprooted and driven downstream during peak runoff.

As the trail begins to enter the narrowing canyon, the landscape changes to a more riparian environment. You will lose sight of the peaks but gain the lush low-lying forests, willows, and grasses that are found along the banks of the river. The hiking can be slow if you need to avoid large obstacles that may be blocking the trail, but the river walk will take you into the back recesses of the canyon and offers the feel of a real wilderness adventure. To return to your vehicle, you will backtrack the same way you came in, noting familiar landmarks from the journey into the canyon.

San Gorgonio Peak, also known as Old Grayback, is the highest point in Southern California

87 *Bogart Park Walkabout*

LENGTH: 4 – 5 miles

HIKING TIME: 3 hours

ELEVATION GAIN: 500 feet

DIFFICULTY: Easy

SEASON: Year-round

INFORMATION: Bogart Park, Beaumont, (909) 845-3818

DIRECTIONS

From Los Angeles or the Palm Springs area, drive on I-10 to Beaumont, a small town 23 miles west of Palm Springs, and turn north on Hwy. 79 (Beaumont Avenue). After about 3 miles turn right at the stop sign indicating Bogart Park to the right. Continue to the next stop sign, then turn left and drive for several miles until you enter the park.

Bogart Park is, for me, one of the real undiscovered treasures of Southern California. Tucked away in the lower San Gorgonio Mountain foothills, this verdant escape offers 414 acres of refreshing flora and fauna that combine the look of "old California" with a mix of cherry trees, elm, pine, and cottonwood suggestive of the hill country of Pennsylvania. All four seasons come to Bogart Park—late March through mid-May is especially inviting, when cherry trees blossom and a light green foliage returns to the trees. Camping, hiking and equestrian trails, some fishing, and an expansive meadow for picnics are available, and a serene out-of-the-way atmosphere pervades the park.

The park is open daily, with a host at the entrance to collect fees on weekends. I often journey here to walk in the cool, quiet morning air as yellow sunbeams illuminate the grasses beneath the groves of California oak. The upper area of the Meadows is another favorite walk of mine, offering glimpses of the western face of towering San Jacinto Mountain to the southeast and the high granite snow-swept face of the San Gorgonio Range to the north. Next to this Meadows section of the park hiking trails lead either around a quiet pond which graces the lower east side, or extend up a nearby hill, accompanied by a rambling stone wall suggestive of Irish country. From the top of the hill, great vistas to the south and west dominate the skyline.

On your own you can follow the Bogart Nature Trail found ⅛ mile past the entrance at the Oaks parking lot. An interpretive brochure is available at the entrance station, pertaining to the trail as it follows along Noble Creek, offering

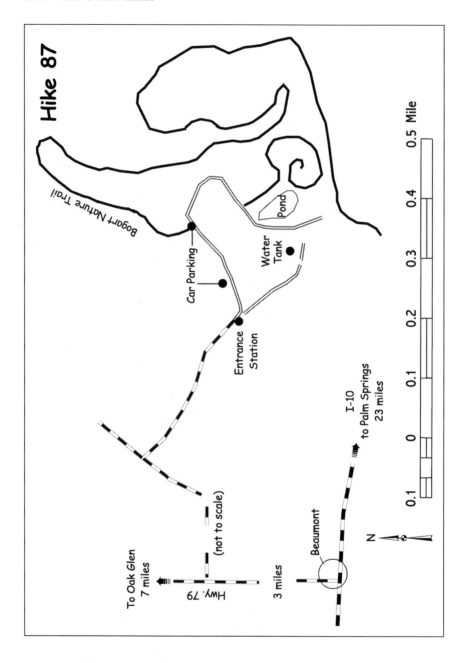

the visitor a look at both riparian and oak woodland habitats. Other hiking trails begin just east of the entrance station and meander into the surrounding hill country. A small trail map is available on weekends at the fee collection station.

You can best experience the true rejuvenating power of Bogart Park alone or with a friend. During the week you'll have the place mostly to yourself. Explore the trails, view the peaceful pastoral settings found throughout the park, and enjoy a picnic lunch in the Meadows. Desert dwellers from the Palm Springs area will find Bogart Park both a cool, refreshing experience, and a glimpse into the magic of the seasons mostly absent from the hot desert environment. After

your visit, return to Hwy. 79, turn right and continue up the mountain 7 miles to Oak Glen, famous for its apples, gourmet foodstuffs, scenic views, and gentle mountain and country people.

Near the upper Meadows section of Bogart Park, hiking trails lead around this quiet pond

88 *Santa Rosa Plateau Walkabout*

LENGTH: 5 – 10 miles

HIKING TIME: 3 – 4 hours

ELEVATION GAIN: 200 feet

DIFFICULTY: Easy/moderate

SEASON: Year-round

INFORMATION: Santa Rosa Ecological Reserve (909) 677-6951

DIRECTIONS

On I-15 drive to Clinton Keith Road, about 10 miles north of Temecula. Turn west (right, if coming down I-15 from Palm Springs or LA) and proceed several miles until you come to the road taking you to the visitor's center.

Another jewel of natural beauty, this plateau invites discovery and offers a serene "old California" setting of chaparral, oak woodlands, and the state's finest remaining bunchgrass prairie. Also located on the reserve is Riverside County's oldest building, an early 1800s adobe ranch house that accents the entire area's ambiance. Here is a glimpse into how California looked before it was settled en masse by the Americans, when old Spanish Land Grant rancheros held sway over the land, and civilization had yet to leave its mark.

Covering almost 7,000 acres, the Santa Rosa Plateau is located at the southern end of the Santa Ana Mountains, just 10 miles north of Temecula. Over 2,000 feet of elevation changes influence the land, with its undisturbed flora, fauna, and habitat, including vernal pools, spring wildflowers, sycamore, willow, and coast live oak trees, sagebrush, California buckwheat, bluegrass prairie, rabbit, coyote, quail, golden eagle, and bobcat. To visit in October or November is to see a twin to the landscape of Northern California's Sonoma and Santa Rosa area, with dried yellow grasslands highlighted by dark green California oak. March and April reveal a lush, verdant explosion of colorful spring wildflowers woven through rolling green prairie, running streams, and rich woodlands. No dogs are permitted on the reserve, and the visitor's center offers brochures about the plateau that day hikers who choose to "walkabout" from trail to trail will find helpful.

Santa Rosa Plateau Preserve offers a landscape of chaparral, oak woodlands, and the state's finest bunchgrass prairie

After parking, pick up a trail map at the visitor's center and walkabout at your own pace and leisure. Many trails loop back on themselves, so the length of your hike is determined only by your time allowance. Early morning is best to view the magnificent surrounding mountain ranges and to absorb the full effect of the area.

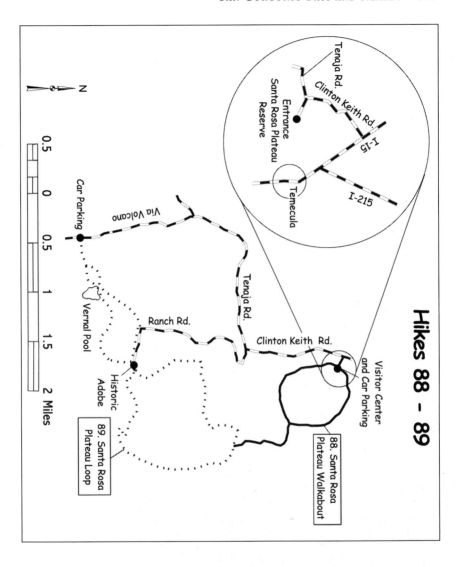

89 *Santa Rosa Plateau Loop*

(see map on page 177)

LENGTH: 9 miles

HIKING TIME: 4 hours

ELEVATION GAIN: 1,000 feet

DIFFICULTY: Moderate/strenuous
"Adventure Hike"

SEASON: Year-round

INFORMATION: Santa Rosa
Ecological Reserve, (909) 677-6951

DIRECTIONS

Follow the directions for Hike 88. Continue on Clinton Keith Road past the visitor's center until you come to the junction of Tenaja and Via Volcano roads. Turn left onto Via Volcano Road until you can see the preserve sign to the left indicating a hiking trail, the Vernal Pool area. Park along the road and hike into the preserve.

In a short while you will come to the Trans Preserve Trail on the left. Turn left onto this trail and proceed for 1.25 miles. As you ramble through the hill country you will be treated to spectacular vistas of the surrounding mountains, the San Gorgonio, Santa Rosa, San Jacinto, and Palomar ranges, made more majestic in early spring if winter snows are still covering the peaks. Spring (mid-March through April) will offer a generous display of wildflowers, including lupine. Some streams will be running, and as you make your way down into the valley, every once in a while your eye will "frame" an incredible picture of pastoral beauty—prairies, mountain backdrops, and green hills that once dominated the Southern California landscape.

In time the trail meets with Hidden Valley Road. Turn right onto this trail/road and follow it past tranquil prairie grasslands where, in places, orange California poppies burst through the green grasslands. After 0.75 mile you will come to the historic adobes, where you can rest, explore the ranch and sur-rounding lands, and picnic on a bench alongside the adobe ranch house. Look inside through the windows for a glimpse of "old California" before resuming your adventure.

The trail continues right of the barn area, indicating the Lomas Trail. In a few yards turn right off the Lomas Trail onto the Adobe Loop Trail, continue through an extended thicket of old oak trees, and follow the somewhat magical-looking flowing stream. The trail continues until it meets with the Punta Trail. In less than a mile this trail junctions with the Mesa Trail. Turn left onto the Mesa Trail as it follows a drainage below the large Mesa de Burro to the right. You will continue climbing along this trail, treated to scenic views of nearby valleys, until connecting with Monument Road. Turn left up the hill, enjoying a vista landscape of the many Southern California mountain ranges that are within easy view of the plateau. At the next junctions, turn left each time until you are back on the Lomas Trail again heading down toward the historic adobes. Once there you can return to your vehicle by heading back on Hidden Valley Road for a short while before meeting the Vernal Pool Trail. Turn left onto this trail and follow it up the ridge for the next mile, then turn right as it tops out and swings back toward where you parked your vehicle. This section of trail can be very flowery in a good spring. Hikers need to take plenty of cool drinks, since the plateau can suddenly warm up, even if the morning starts off cool.

This early 1800s adobe ranch house is the oldest building in Riverside County

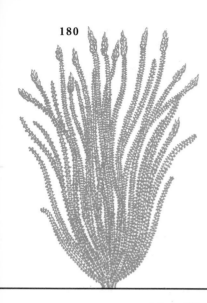

Orocopia Mountain Wilderness and the Chuckwalla Mountains

Hikes 90 – 100

Trailhead Locations in the Orocopia Mountain Wilderness and the Chuckwalla Mountains (Hikes 90 - 100)

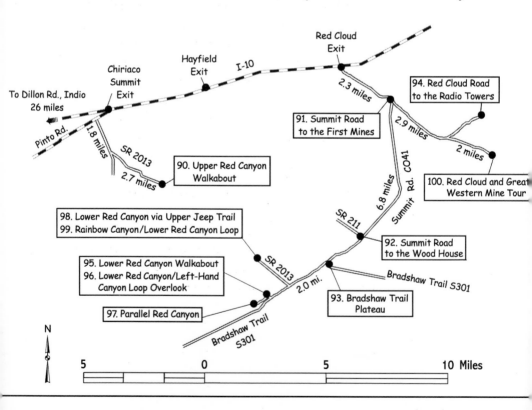

Gold fever struck the Colorado River Basin south of Blythe, California, in the early 1860s near La Paz, Arizona. For shipment supplies from the coast, the Bradshaw Road was constructed through both the Orocopia and Chuckwalla mountains. The road still exists, now known as the Bradshaw Trail, and provides 4WD enthusiasts a jeep road just north of the Salton Sea that leads all the way to Arizona.

The name Orocopia is Spanish for "much gold." The mountains east of Box Canyon, stretching 25 miles to the Bradshaw Road, are these Orocopia Mountains . . . minus any real gold. A scattering of played-out mines dots the landscape, but the real "treasure" is the wilderness experience this area affords hikers who want to access a spot in Southern California that still hints of the Old West.

To my knowledge the trail descriptions in this book are the most extensive yet written about this area. From the very first time I headed into this wilderness, I knew that I had found a place to rejuvenate and release the cares of the world— a place where I could feel like a visitor to a far-off time when the thrill of being the first person to visit "somewhere new" was still a possibility. The Red Canyon area suggests southern Utah and Moab like no other place in California. The plateau valley separating the Orocopia and Chuckwalla mountains offers spectacular vistas of multiple mountain ranges, mysterious rocky upthrusts to the east, and grand shimmering "blue mountains" on the far southern horizon . . . a visual sweep of almost 100 miles. The land itself draws you into it in such a way that the "child explorer" in each of us joyfully surfaces and delights in the clean open spaces. Exotic winding canyons, abandoned old mines, red rock formations, and a vast openness that stretches to colorful mountains on every horizon are reason enough to brave the elements and discover the Orocopia Wilderness and Chuckwalla Mountains for yourself!

Most of the "trails" are in fact jeep trails, with considerable opportunities for off-trail rambles into endless canyons and mountain recesses. The hiker just needs to mentally mark his or her return. October and November yield blue autumn skies, and in a wet year, March and April surprise the visitor with abundant and rare flowers, ocotillo in bloom, yellow-flowering palo verde trees, multitudes of ironwood trees, desert tortoise, and red-tailed hawk.

90 *Upper Red Canyon Walkabout*

LENGTH: 8 miles

HIKING TIME: 4 hours

ELEVATION GAIN: 200 feet

DIFFICULTY: Easy/moderate

SEASON: October to April

INFORMATION: BLM Office, Palm Springs, (760) 251-4800

Red Canyon cuts through the eastern section of the Orocopia Mountain Wilderness and offers the hiker entry from both the north or south. This northern route shows the hiker hints of the more stunning red rock formations found at the southern end of the canyon, and it offers majestic vistas of the valley to the east.

Beginning as a jeep trail, the Upper Red Canyon hike climbs to an abundance of interesting rock formations

DIRECTIONS

Take I-10 east 26 miles from the Dillon Road exit just beyond Indio to the Chiriaco Summit turnoff. Turn off the freeway at the stop sign on the right, then right again on Pinto Road heading west for almost a mile. Turn left at the dirt road with a sign located several yards from the road. Off-road vehicles, jeeps, and trucks are recommended for accessing the trailhead. Passenger cars can reach the trailhead but only after a rough ride. Drive on the dirt road for 1.8 miles, noting the signpost to the right indicating Red Canyon Road/Trail, also designated SR 2013. Stay on the obvious main road as it makes its way after another 2.7 miles directly into the mountains. Park just before the road drops down into a wash.

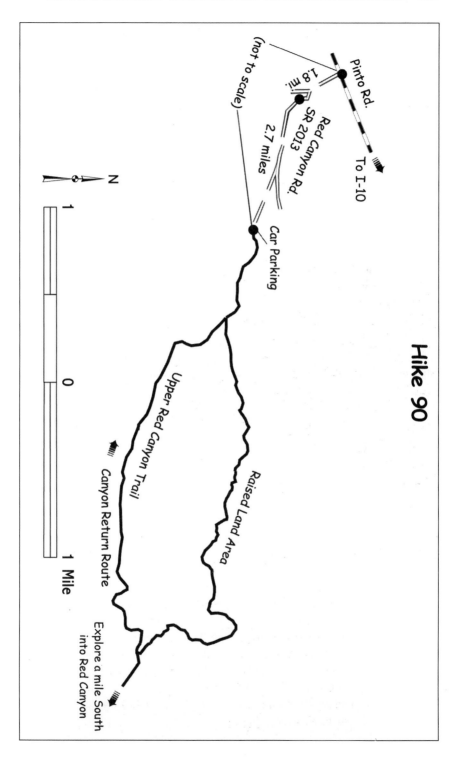

Hike 90

Pinto Rd.

To I-10

1.8 mi.

Red Canyon Rd.
SR 2013

2.7 miles

(not to scale)

Car Parking

N

1   0   1 Mile

Upper Red Canyon Trail

Raised Land Area

Canyon Return Route

Explore a mile South
into Red Canyon

The hike follows this jeep trail for several miles, climbing onto raised land areas where quartz rock is abundant. Indeed, these mountains are awash in interesting mineral specimens, so keep a sharp eye out for another favorite rock to collect! When the trail leads you into a small canyon, it will take a turn up and out of the canyon and, in another mile-plus, lead you above a large canyon to your right—Red Canyon. Here I suggest you drop down into Red Canyon and explore it heading south (left) for a mile or so. Return north through the canyon and you will eventually intersect the same trail you hiked in on.

Throughout the hike a good roving eye will spot many nearby side trails that beg for exploring. Note, too, the geology of Upper Red Canyon and how it differs radically from that of Lower Red Canyon.

91 *Summit Road to the First Mines*

LENGTH: 6 miles

HIKING TIME: 3 hours

ELEVATION GAIN: 150 feet

DIFFICULTY: Easy

SEASON: October to April

INFORMATION: BLM Office, Palm Springs, (760) 251-4800

This hike leads to several abandoned mines in the northeastern portion of the Orocopia Mountains. It also offers many side canyons that the more curious hiker might explore.

DIRECTIONS

From the Dillon Road exit just beyond Indio, take I-10 east for 35 miles and continue to Red Cloud Road exit, the second exit east past Chiriaco Summit. Turn right onto Red Cloud Road, right at the stop sign, then 0.3 mile to the wide jeep road to the left. This dirt jeep road is one of the main access roads into the Orocopia Mountain Wilderness. Passenger cars can negotiate this road but will experience a bumpy washboard ride. At this northern terminus of Red Cloud Road, look for the large map sign to the right of the road.

Continue 2.3 miles south along this road until you come to the junction where the road splits into three. Take the middle fork, known as CO Road 41 or Summit Road. Just as you ease onto this road, take a sharp turn down the road to the right, crossing the railroad tracks, and park in the large flat area just off the road to your left.

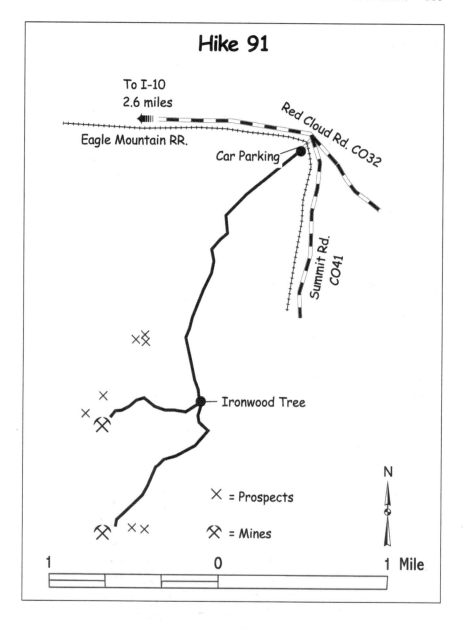

Hike 91

To I-10
2.6 miles

Red Cloud Rd. CO32

Eagle Mountain RR.

Car Parking

Summit Rd. CO41

⨉⨂

Ironwood Tree

⨉

⨉

⨂

⨉ = Prospects

⨂

⨉⨉

⨂ = Mines

N

1   0   1 Mile

Hikers follow Summit Road into the Orocopia Wilderness

Begin your hike west on this dirt road for almost 2 miles until you come to a large wash. Be sure to stay left, as the road splits to the right 0.5 mile from the wash. Just before entering the wash, note the side trail branching off to the left and crossing the wash just left of a large ironwood tree. Follow this trail as it crosses the wash and then becomes a jeep trail winding into the backcountry, which is filled with exotic mountains. This road/trail leads farther into the mountains for almost a mile, with great vistas of the Eagle and Coxcomb Mountains to the northeast. The trail continues above and into a canyon wash, with opportunities to explore several inviting canyons to the left of the trail. Eventually the trail ends at the base of a mining area. Climbing up the side of the excavations and remaining woodworks, hikers may get lucky and view some artifacts from an earlier day.

To reach the second mine, retrace your steps to where the trail enters the first wash at the large ironwood tree. Turn left down the wash and bushwhack along the wash as it winds its way around and into the nearby mountains. In less than a mile you will see the trail leading left up to another abandoned mining area.

This easy exploratory adventure gives one the feeling of always being on the verge of some great discovery, and in March and April, after a wet winter, the landscape is surprisingly green with flowers, bushes, and trees, especially the palo verde. Time of day can impact the aesthetics of this hike; I recommend early morning, especially since it warms up to the 80s by midday in spring.

92 *Summit Road to the Wood House* (see map on page 188)

LENGTH: 10 miles

HIKING TIME: 4 – 5 hours

ELEVATION GAIN: 100 feet

DIFFICULTY: Moderate

SEASON: October to April

INFORMATION: BLM Office, Palm Springs, (760) 251-4800

This hike crosses a wide desert plain and ends in the eastern fringe of the Orocopia Mountains, where a lone wooden house structure stands and where an interesting canyon leads into the back recesses of the foothills.

DIRECTIONS

Follow the directions for Hike 91. After turning off I-10 and onto Red Cloud Road, drive south and turn onto Summit Road. Then continue another 6.8 miles until you come to SR 211 (Amy's Wash Road) and park just after turning onto it.

The hike follows Amy's Wash Road 5 miles across desert flatlands into the mountains. You are treated to magnificent 360 degree sweeps of the Orocopia/Chuckwalla Basin, nearby mountains, and often noisy flyby practice runs by F-14/F-16 fighter jets. As you cross the wide, upsweeping valley, note the change

Railroad tracks lead into the Orocopia Wilderness

in vegetation. I have spotted desert tortoise along this route as well as beautiful flowering ocotillo bushes. After 5 miles you will spot an old wooden structure just west of the trail. This property is to be looked at only and its privacy respected.

However, you are free to roam up to the nearby mountains and look for signs of past mining activity.

Continue southwest/west on the main trail. It will curve around the mountain and in less than 0.5 mile will take you above an interesting canyon before abruptly ending at the base of the foothills. This area invites exploration and gives you the feeling of isolation in a place "all your own."

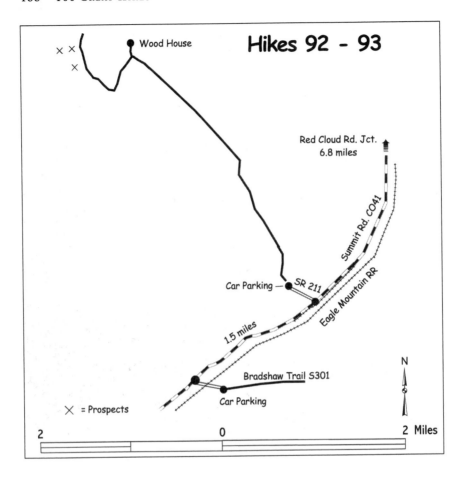

Hikes 92 - 93

Wood House

Red Cloud Rd. Jct.
6.8 miles

Summit Rd. CO41

Car Parking — SR 211

Eagle Mountain RR

1.5 miles

Bradshaw Trail S301

Car Parking

N

✕ = Prospects

2   0   2 Miles

93 *Bradshaw Trail Plateau*

LENGTH: 10 miles

HIKING TIME: 4 – 5 hours

ELEVATION GAIN: 150 feet

DIFFICULTY: Easy/moderate

SEASON: October to April

INFORMATION: BLM Office, Palm Springs, (760) 251-4800

DIRECTIONS
Follow the road directions for Hike 91. After reaching Summit Road, drive south on this road for 8.3 miles until you reach Bradshaw Trail marker S301. A map sign is to your right, but you can park in any accessible spots.

This hike takes you along a section of the Bradshaw Trail that crosses between the Orocopia and Chuckwalla mountains east toward Arizona. It offers a pleasant meander up the plateau, just north of the Chocolate Mountains Bombing Range, with beautiful views of the entire valley looking west. This hike is especially nice if you want to just "get away" to some far isolated spot that opens wide to the four horizons and doesn't tax your stamina.

Red Canyon viewed from the Bradshaw Trail

Begin the hike by hiking east on the Bradshaw Trail, which turns left off Summit Road. The trail slowly climbs above the valley, offering wide, expansive vistas of the entire valley and surrounding mountains. You will cross several washes along the way, and you may see desert tortoise. In a wet winter, flowering species of trees and bushes can be found along the route.

After 3 miles look right for the remains of old fuel pods and "bomblike" used devices.

The trail continues east for 50 miles before reaching Arizona, so your turn-around spot will be at your own discretion and desire to explore along the trail.

Do honor the signs that caution you away from the adjacent bombing range. On any given day you might also be buzzed by naval fighter jets on a training mission in the area.

94 Red Cloud Road to the Radio Towers

LENGTH: 5 miles

HIKING TIME: 3 hours

ELEVATION GAIN: 1,700 feet

DIFFICULTY: Strenuous

SEASON: October to April

INFORMATION: BLM Office, Palm Springs, (760) 251-4800

This hike challenges you with a straight-up workout, with some grades approaching 30 percent. You will follow a jeep road to the top of a mountain, where a large array of radio towers relays signals from across Southern California. The view at the top is magnificent and well worth the sweat; however, the "trail" is not the easiest to climb up or down!

DIRECTIONS   Follow the directions for Hike 91, but after reaching Red Cloud Road where the sign shows the map of the area, continue south on the dirt road 2.6 miles to where Summit Road veers right off Red Cloud Road. Stay on Red Cloud Road, the left road, for another 2.9 miles to where the road splits again. Passenger cars can travel this road, but with difficulty. I recommend a 4WD vehicle or a truck. Take the road to the left that heads east toward the radio tower mountain, and park at the base of the mountain where convenient.

From here the dirt road/trail leads straight up to the top of the mountain, with several 30 percent grades that will have you slip-sliding your way up the steep incline. You'll get great views on the way up, but once you're at the top of the mountain, make your way around the towers for a spectacular vista overlook of the Chuckwalla and Orocopia mountains, a view that just may include Arizona to the east. When I hiked this road I was passed by a service truck that gave me a friendly hello, so I believe the road is accessible to hikers. Of course, respectful treatment of the property at the top is a given. This strenuous workout is challenging enough to entice only the most sturdy of hikers.

The distant Radio Towers are at the top of this peak

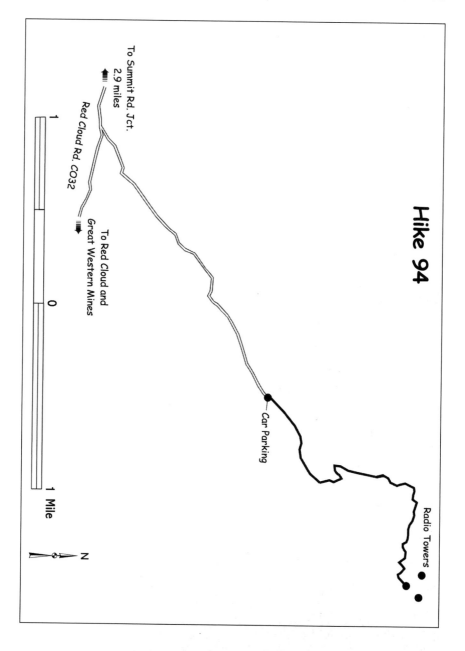

Hike 94

95 *Lower Red Canyon Walkabout*

LENGTH: 4 – 6 miles

HIKING TIME: 3 – 4 hours

ELEVATION GAIN: 0 feet

DIFFICULTY: Easy

SEASON: October to April

INFORMATION: BLM Office, Palm Springs, (760) 251-4800

This hike takes you to the heart of the Orocopia Mountain Wilderness, the large 10- to 12-mile long canyon known as Red Canyon. This area is highlighted by a parallel system of canyons more suggestive of the Moab, Utah, red rock country than any place in Southern California. A network of jeep and hiking trails crisscrosses the canyon area, allowing side trips during a long hike to at least one other adjacent canyon.

DIRECTIONS Follow the road directions for Hike 91. Once on Summit Road, drive south 10.6 miles to the signpost marked Red Canyon. The entrance to the canyon is marked by a massive rock cliff formation. Drive into the canyon and park.

Begin this walkabout hike by first looking onto the cliff face to your right as you enter Red Canyon. You can easily spot a large red-tailed hawk's nest three-quarters of the way up the cliff. Continue hiking into the canyon and you will

The Red Canyon, nearly 12 miles in length, is at the heart of the Orocopia Mountain Wilderness

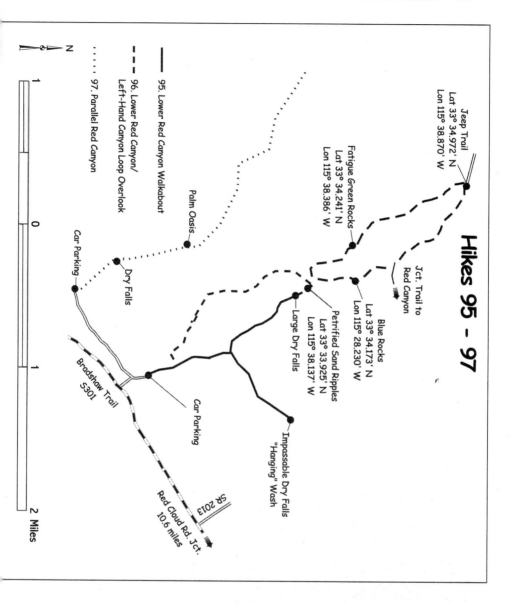

be able to examine a generous spring offering of flowers if winter rains were adequate. Desert tortoise have also been spotted in the bush areas near the canyon entrance.

After 0.75 mile the canyon splits, with a large canyon branch veering left (do not follow the smaller branches found during the first 0.25 mile). Follow this branch into a beautiful canyon where soft sculptured sand cliffs create a mystical landscape, highlighted by several "sand towers" along the way and many small side canyons that invite exploring but do not lead far from the main branch canyon.

You will come to a large dry falls on your right after 0.75 mile. The trail continues to the left and eventually to several jeep trails leading steeply out of the canyon. This marks your turn-around spot. Return down canyon to the main section of Red Canyon, turn left, and walk up the canyon for another 0.75 mile until you reach a huge dry falls and "hanging wash" that blocks any further hiking on this route. Return to your vehicle the same way you came in.

96 Lower Red Canyon/Left-Hand Canyon Loop Overlook *(see map on page 193)*

LENGTH: 8 miles

HIKING TIME: 4 hours

ELEVATION GAIN: 800 feet

DIFFICULTY: Moderate/strenuous "Adventure Hike"

SEASON: October to April

INFORMATION: BLM Office, Palm Springs, (760) 251-4800

DIRECTIONS   Follow the directions for Hike 95.

This hike has it all. It first takes you into and then above Red Canyon; drops you down into a spectacular uplifted colorful rock canyon that looks more like Moab, Utah; takes you out of this canyon and back again above Red Canyon; drops back down into the colorful rock canyon, through massive stratified uplifted rock; and finally goes back through a side branch of Red Canyon.

As you enter Red Canyon, hike for 0.25 mile until you come to the first small canyon to the left. Follow the trail up this canyon as it climbs the ridge to the south of Red Canyon. After 45 minutes of steady hiking, climbing ever higher hill crests, you will turn down and right off the ridge trail you've been following. Along this trail section you will be treated to spectacular vistas of the Red Canyon area, colorful explosions of rock outcroppings throughout the low mountains and hills to the south, views of the parallel canyons south of Red Canyon and—on clear days—even Salton Sea.

Hike down off the ridge trail, following a jeep trail to the left for 0.25 mile until it drops down into a beautiful red rock Utah-like canyon I call Left-Hand Canyon, because it lies just left (south) of Red Canyon proper. Colorful red, mauve, lilac, robin's egg blue, amber, and rust rock strata highlight this canyon and invite rock examinations often along the way.

As you drop down into the canyon, hike left up the canyon wash for a mile or more until you come to a jeep trail climbing out of the canyon to your right. (Do not take the jeep trails near where you first dropped down into the canyon.)

Climb out of Left-Hand Canyon up the steep jeep trail, noting the magnificent rock and canyon formations to the south and west. Hike down the other side of the hill to the jeep trail found at the bottom of the hill. Turn right, while enjoying the abundant mix of rocks found along this ridge portion of the hike.

Continue for 0.5 mile east along the ridge trail until the trail turns sharply to the left toward Red Canyon. Quickly turn to your right and bushwhack 40 yards to the fainter ridge trail that hugs the northern section of Left-Hand Canyon, following along but above the same canyon wash you hiked in on.

Follow this ridge trail, always staying to your far right just in from the canyon's edge, until you come to a light blue mass of broken rock pieces along the trail, about 0.5 mile from where you left the last jeep trail as you headed down into Red Canyon. Follow the sliver trail heading down 30 yards until widening into a faint jeep trail. Follow this trail just before it turns very steeply down into Left-Hand Canyon, almost at the exact place you first entered the canyon from the jeep trail above and south of the canyon. For a safer descent, negotiate the small rock wash leading down into Left-Hand Canyon, found just right of the steeper jeep trail.

Along this trail, hikers enjoy spectacular vistas of the Red Canyon area and—on a clear day—the Salton Sea

Once in the canyon, turn left and enjoy a section of uplifted red rock strata, narrow canyon slots, and small dry waterfalls until you come to a massive, large drop of dry falls. Veer left around and down the rock face onto the canyon floor, and turn left. Sand cliffs and sculptured towers accent the canyon for the next 0.75 mile until it empties into Red Canyon. Turn right and follow the canyon back to your vehicle.

97 *Parallel Red Canyon*
(see map on page 193)

LENGTH: 8 miles

HIKING TIME: 4 hours

ELEVATION GAIN: 300 feet

DIFFICULTY: Moderate

SEASON: October to April

INFORMATION: BLM Office, Palm Springs, (760) 251-4800

DIRECTIONS

After following the route for Hike 95, turn left at the first signpost, just before entering Red Canyon. This dirt jeep road runs alongside the canyons for 0.8 mile until you can enter the first canyon on your right. This I call Parallel Red Canyon, because it parallels Red Canyon and offers spectacular red rock formations.

After entering the canyon, park your vehicle. Proceed up canyon. Note the rich, exotic rock formations along the way, especially the abundant quartz deposits located in cracks in red rock strata. After 0.5 mile you will encounter

Rock formations in Parallel Red Canyon strongly resemble the red rock country of Moab, Utah

a small, uplifted dry falls, which looks like it was actually built from cement. Continue hiking the canyon floor as it climbs slowly up canyon. After a mile you will come to a palm oasis where above, on both sides of the canyon, a light greenish rock strata erupts from the rock surface.

Further hiking takes you over several uplifted rock formations, but the main feature of Parallel Red Canyon remains the stunning red strata accented here and there by lilac, bluish-green, and rust-colored rock. If you feel energetic and curious enough, try bushwhacking over the canyon to gain a vista, or following the many branch canyons off to the left. As long as you know where you are in relation to Parallel Red Canyon, your land navigation skills will lead you safely back to your vehicle.

98 *Lower Red Canyon via Upper Jeep Trail*

LENGTH: 8 miles

HIKING TIME: 4 hours

ELEVATION GAIN: 500 feet

DIFFICULTY: Moderate

SEASON: October to April

INFORMATION: BLM Office, Palm Springs, (760) 251-4800

The jeep trail designated SR 2013 climbs above Lower Red Canyon's north ridge for better than 10 miles, offering great vistas of the Orocopia Mountain Wilderness along the way while providing "side jeep trails" down into Red Canyon for exploration of the canyon bottom.

DIRECTIONS
Follow the directions for Hike 95. After 10.3 miles, Summit Road meets SR 2013, the jeep trail that travels along the north ridge of Lower Red Canyon. Turn right off Summit Road and onto Red Canyon Jeep Trail SR 2013. Park where it's convenient, perhaps 0.25 mile in from the road.

The trail climbs the ridge above Red Canyon, sometimes quite steeply, while offering several side jeep trails down into Red Canyon to the left of the ridge trail. Hike for almost 2 miles before taking the left jeep trail (the third signpost you come to) down into Red Canyon. The trail is very steep, so caution going down and up is advisable. Once you're at the bottom, turn left for 0.5 mile until you come to the high drop-off that stops any further hiking down canyon. This severe drop leaves part of Red Canyon on a "higher shelf," while isolating a lower section that leads back to Summit Road. Explore up canyon in a westerly direction before returning to your vehicle via the upper ridge trail.

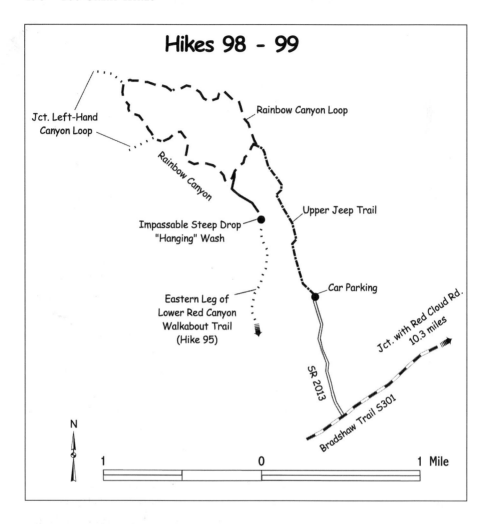

Hikes 98 - 99

Jct. Left-Hand
Canyon Loop

Rainbow Canyon Loop

Rainbow Canyon

Impassable Steep Drop
"Hanging" Wash

Upper Jeep Trail

Eastern Leg of
Lower Red Canyon
Walkabout Trail
(Hike 95)

Car Parking

Jct. with Red Cloud Rd.
10.3 miles

SR 2013

Bradshaw Trail S301

N

1   0   1 Mile

The Orocopia Mountains are just visible from above Red Canyon

Lower Red Canyon resembles the red rock country of southern Utah. Many spectacular side canyons branch off the main canyon floor, leading to exotic and colorful rock formations. Explore at your own leisure. The climb back out will be very steep and slippery, so caution is advisable.

99 Rainbow Canyon/ Lower Red Canyon Loop

LENGTH: 7 miles

HIKING TIME: 3 – 4 hours

ELEVATION GAIN: 500 feet

DIFFICULTY: Moderate

SEASON: October to April

INFORMATION: BLM Office, Palm Springs, (760) 251-4800

DIRECTIONS Follow the directions for Hike 98.

Once parked, begin hiking on the jeep trail SR 2013 as it quickly climbs the north ridge above Red Canyon. During the next several miles the trail gradually rises, sometimes in steep upgrades, until leveling out on the north ridge of Red Canyon. Along the way you will view the entire Orocopia Basin as well as the pronounced, colorful surrounding mountain ranges. On a clear day you can also observe the deep blue ribbon of the Salton Sea to the south.

After almost 2 miles you will come to a signpost marking a left turn off the ridge trail and down into Red Canyon. (Any other signposts before 2 miles should not be followed.) This is the third signpost you come to. As you look south toward the southern edge of Lower Red Canyon, notice the colorful explosion of light green, red, and dark mauve rocks. This marks the part of Rainbow Canyon where you will soon be hiking.

The jeep trail down into Red Canyon is steep, so caution is advisable. Once you're on the canyon floor, turn right and note the small canyon with a narrow opening ahead on your left, branching off Red Canyon. This seemingly insignificant canyon holds a beautiful treasure of multicolored—almost rainbowlike—rocks and rock strata . . . Rainbow Canyon.

Hike slowly up this canyon, making your way in a stair-step fashion, examining the many colorful rock layers and individual rocks as you hike. Keep to the right, negotiating any short dry falls that you come to. The canyon winds up and westward for less than 0.5 mile. When the canyon truly ends, bushwhack up the left side until you gain the farthest, highest ridge. Hike farther south across the slope until you come to the next ridge of the next major canyon. There you will find your trail, a faint path/old jeep road. Turn right.

Hike west for 1 mile until the trail joins a very developed jeep trail veering down and to the right toward Red Canyon and away from the ridge you have just hiked along. Note the spectacularly colored rock formations nearby and in the mountains farther to the south. This developed jeep trail makes its way down into Red Canyon, where you will turn right and hike another mile before you get to the jeep trail that climbs left out of the canyon and back to your vehicle along the ridge trail you came in on. This climb out is steep and slippery, so use caution.

100   *Red Cloud and Great Western Mine Tour*

LENGTH: 7 miles

HIKING TIME: 4 hours

ELEVATION GAIN: 300 feet

DIFFICULTY: Moderate

SEASON: October to April

INFORMATION: BLM Office, Palm Springs, (760) 251-4800

Although the Spanish name for this area, the Orocopia Mountain Wilderness, means "much gold," little gold was ever taken out of the Orocopias in the period between 1860 and 1930. However, several mines operated on the Chuckwalla Mountain side of the wilderness in the early part of the twentieth century. These were the Red Cloud and Great Western Mines. Only scattered remains mark the land that once supported a serious mining concern. The hike into the mining area is both scenic and hints at the romantic, nostalgic flavor of the "Old West"

DIRECTIONS Follow the directions for Hike 91. When Summit Road junctions with Red Cloud Road, continue left on Red Cloud Road CO32 for 2.9 miles until you come to the split in the road. Veer right at the signpost to stay on Red Cloud Road and continue driving for another 2 miles until you come to a wide turnout parking area to the right. Park there. Continue by hiking south on the road you drove in on.

The hike takes you into a canyon area that narrows after 0.5 mile. The trail leads past an old stone and cement structure that could have been a stamping mill. Other stone structures can be found on the left side of the canyon nearby. After another mile-plus, the trail follows the jeep road into the canyon where you will begin encountering your first "old mine" remains of Red Cloud Mine. To your right you'll see a cyanide leaching pit. Explore the trail going left off the main trail as it climbs a road to reveal several large slag piles with some old rusted iron structures still standing.

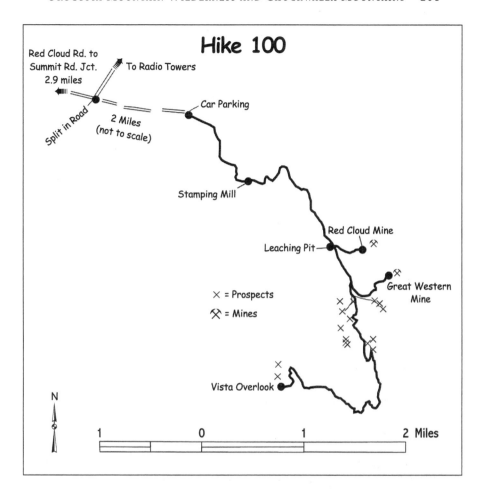

Return to the main trail and hike another 0.5 mile until you come to the Great Western Mine. Numerous side trails up into the surrounding hills and along canyon bottoms offer adventure seekers plenty of opportunities for discovering the extent

of this once large mining operation. A bushwhack 0.5 mile farther into the canyon due south will reveal a trail to the right which climbs into the mountains and ends in a spectacular vista overlook of the whole Orocopia Mountain Wilderness Basin.

Ruins from twentieth-century mining operations dot the landscape near Red Cloud Mine

Appendix 1
Hikes According to Degree of Difficulty

Easy Hikes

Miles		Hike Number
5	Painted Canyon/Ladder Canyon Loop	1
5	Little Painted Canyon Walkabout	2
6	Pushawalla Palms and Canyon Trail	8
3	Willis Palms and West Mesa Trail	9
6	Coachella Valley Preserve Trails	10
2	Andreas Canyon	25
4	Earl Henderson Trail	28
5	The Ernie Maxwell Scenic Trail	37
3	Hurkey Creek Trail	47
5	Horsethief Creek via Cactus Spring Trail	62
3	Santa Rosa Mountain Road to Toro Peak	65
1	Barker Dam Loop	72
3	Big Morongo Canyon Preserve Walkabout	83
5	Bogart Park Walkabout	87
6	Summit Road to the First Mines	91
6	Lower Red Canyon Walkabout	95

Moderate Hikes

Miles		Hike Number
5	Little and Big Painted Canyon/Ladders Loop	3
5	Box Canyon's "The Grottos" Cave Hike	4
5	Box Canyon 1st Grotto Loop to Hidden Springs	5
6	Eisenhower Peak Loop	15
6	Carrizo Canyon	16
8	Palm Canyon Trail to Lost Paradise	19
8	Palm Canyon Trail to Bullseye Rock	20
6	Murray Canyon Trail	22
7	Shannon Trail Loop	29
6	The Araby Trail	30

Moderate Hikes *(continued)*

Strenuous Hikes

Strenuous Hikes *(continued)*

Strenuous Hikes *(continued)*

Miles		Hike Number
22	Agua Alta Spring	64
18	Sawmill Road Trail/Toro Peak	66
16	Palm Canyon Pines-to-Palms Trail	67
11	South Fork of the Pacific Crest Trail	68
12	Long Canyon to Chuckawalla Bill's Ruins	69
10	Eureka Peak Loop	70
8	Carey's Castle	75
14	Pinkham Canyon Walkabout	77
14	Pipes Canyon Toward Big Bear	80
9	San Bernardino Peak Trail to Columbine Spring	81
10	Pacific Crest Trail South from I-10	84
12	Mission Creek to Whitewater River Canyon Walkabout	86
5	Red Cloud Road to the Radio Towers	94

Appendix 2
Special Hikes — Full Moon, Flowers, Families

Best Full Moon Hikes

These trails offer an easy hike for full moon trekking, and should be limited to just the first 2-3 miles of the hike before you turn around:

Mecca Hills/Box Canyon:　#1, Painted Canyon/Ladder Canyon Loop
　　　　　　　　　　　　#4, Box Canyon's "The Grottos" Cave Hike

San Jacinto Mountains:　#50, Spitler Peak Trail
　　　　　　　　　　　#52, Thomas Mountain East Road to Summit
　　　　　　　　　　　#57, North Fork of the Pacific Crest Trail to
　　　　　　　　　　　　　Live Oak Spring

Santa Rosa Mountains:　#66, Sawmill Road Trail/Toro Peak (first 2 miles)
　　　　　　　　　　　#67, Palm Canyon Pines-to-Palms Trail (first 3 miles)
　　　　　　　　　　　#68, South Fork of the Pacific Crest Trail

Best Spring Flower Hikes

Flowers in spring are often seen in large quantities only in a truly wet year, one with 6-plus inches of rain. These trails offer easy hikes to view some great floral displays, provided adequate moisture has occurred:

Mecca Hills/Box Canyon: #4, Box Canyon's "The Grottos" Cave Hike

Joshua Tree National Park: #76, Lost Palms Oasis Trail at
Cottonwood Spring

San Gorgonio Pass and Nearby: #78, Pipes Canyon Loop
#82, Big Morongo Canyon Trail
#85, Mission Creek to the Pacific Crest Trail North
#88, Santa Rosa Plateau Walkabout

Best Family Hikes with Kids

Mecca Hills/Box Canyon: #1, Painted Canyon/Ladder Canyon Loop
#3, Little and Big Painted Canyon/Ladders Loop
#4, Box Canyon's "The Grottos" Cave Hike

Coachella Preserve: #10, Coachella Valley Preserve Trails

Palm Springs and
Indian Canyons: #25, Andreas Canyon

San Jacinto Mountains: #37, The Ernie Maxwell Scenic Trail
#47, Hurkey Creek Trail

Santa Rosa Mountains: #62, Horsethief Creek via Cactus Spring Trail

Joshua Tree National Park: #72, Barker Dam Loop

San Gorgonio Pass and Nearby: #83, Big Morongo Canyon Preserve Walkabout
#87, Bogart Park Walkabout
#88, Santa Rosa Plateau Walkabout

Orocopia Mountain Wilderness
and the Chuckwalla Mountains: #95, Lower Red Canyon Walkabout
#97, Parallel Red Canyon

Appendix 3
Best Restaurants After a Hike

For years members of the Coachella Valley Hiking Club and I have fellow-shipped after a hike with either a late lunch or early dinner at restaurants that welcome hikers after a long day on the trail. We have appreciated considerate and fast service and the most excellent food for weary hikers with big appetites. If you are planning a lunch or dinner with a larger group, or to ensure timely seating, call ahead and find the times of operation and seating availability. Here are my best recommendations for fine restaurants that welcome hikers and whose food is exceptionally good:

Santa Rosa Mountains hikes:
SUGARLOAF CAFE, 70111 Hwy. 74, Mountain Center, (760) 349-9020.
   Great food, very friendly to hikers, comfortable setting.

Idyllwild and San Jacinto Mountains hikes:
THE GASTROGNOME RESTAURANT, 54381 Ridgeview Dr., Idyllwild,
   (909) 659-5055. A real "five star" presentation of fine dining, warm
   mountain atmosphere.

Banning Pass area hikes:
 A & W ROOTBEER, Cabazon, (909) 849-3301. A '50s-style restaurant with
   great food and fast service.

All hikes east and south of Indio:
CIRO'S RISTORANTE & PIZZERIA, 81-963 Hwy. 11, Indio, (760) 347-6503.
   Pizza, lasagna, great food, great service.
TERESA'S CAFE, 45-682 Towne St., Indio, (760) 347-7411. The best Mexican
   home-cooked meals!

Yucca Valley/Joshua Tree National Park hikes:
DIN HO CHINESE RESTAURANT, 56-098 29 Palms Hwy., Yucca Valley,
   (760) 365-4353. Chinese food at its best, comfortable atmosphere, and
   fast service.

Appendix 4
Differential Correction of GPS Fixes

When the Global Positioning System (GPS) was first put in place, the U.S. Government was concerned about the security of the military operations that were to be the prime beneficiaries of the system. The concern was that an enemy could utilize the high accuracy of the GPS system to target U.S. forces in the field or knock out U.S. defense systems.

In order to thwart this possibility, purposeful errors were introduced in the satellite clocks. This in turn causes random range errors in position computations. Although 95 percent of the time the error is small, 5 percent of the time it can be as much as 100 yards. The user never knows just which amount of error is in place at a given time. This process is known as Selective Availability (SA).

Theoretically, SA prohibits an enemy agent from accurately pinpointing a target unless the random range errors can be eliminated in real time. Unless the agent has access to the right equipment, this will not be possible.

Differential correction is the procedure by which the random range errors are removed. There are two methods for accomplishing this correction.

Real Time Differential Correction

For reasons that will quickly become clear, this method is great for boats or vehicles but not practical for hikers.

The Coast Guard provides a correction signal that can be received via a 300 kHz radio receiver. The signal is applied to the fix that the GPS receiver has just computed. The receiver retails for about $300 and needs a bunch of batteries—heavy ones—to power it. It's great for finding your way into a harbor in a fog but impractical for a hiker who wants to carry a pack with a reasonable weight. This method is accurate to about 15 feet and is in real time. This can be crucial to a skipper entering a rocky harbor, but does a hiker really have to be that fussy?

Past Processed Differential Correction

The GPS fixes shown on the maps in this book were corrected using this method.

There are several locations in the United States that record SA error every few seconds and post this information on the Internet. To use this data, you will require a special GPS receiver. This instrument will record the satellite data and time-tag each fix as you move along the trail.

At home you can download the data from the GPS receiver into your computer. Proprietary software is available to allow access to the information posted on the Internet. After you have processed the data, the resultant fixes will be accurate to one yard. This all assumes that you found your way successfully and got home to indulge in a little techno-geek activity!

Trimble is one of several manufacturers of high-end GPS equipment and proprietary software. If you want more information about GPS or differential correction, visit the Trimble website on the Internet at www.trimble.com.

Appendix 5
Helpful Hiking Hints for Desert Visitors

Palm Springs Aerial Tramway

Palm Springs Aerial Tramway gets you to the top of the San Jacinto Mountains/ Mount San Jacinto State Park. The tram runs most of the year and affords desert visitors a quick and scenic ride to the mountain trails above Palm Springs. A restaurant is also featured, with a ranger station just outside the Mountain Tram Station. By riding the tram, hikers can take longer hikes instead of spending valuable time driving. Please check with the tram for additional information at (760) 325-1391 or (760) 327-6002; www.pstramway.com. The tram is located on Hwy. 111, just at the northern edge of town.

Weather

Hikers should be aware that early morning temperatures, especially after March 1 and before November 1, can be deceptive. Temperatures of 60-70 degrees at the trailhead can soon become 85-100 by afternoon. Always take a generous supply of cold drinks, 1 quart per 4 miles hiked.

Also, the temperatures in the Santa Rosa and San Jacinto mountains can be 40–50 degrees cooler than the desert floor, especially if a cold, moist marine layer of clouds has penetrated into the mountains and a strong, onshore flow or breeze is present.

Dirt Jeep Roads

All of the roads into the Orocopia Mountain Wilderness and Painted Canyon/Mecca Hills are dirt jeep roads. If in doubt, contact the Bureau of Land Management at (760) 251-4800 to see if they are passable. Passenger cars usually can access the trails into Painted Canyon/Box Canyon, and along Red Cloud Road, Summit Road, and portions of Bradshaw Trail in the Orocopias.

Unmarked Trails and Signs

Most desert trails in the Coachella Valley are either not marked at the trailhead or marked sparingly along the way. This requires hikers to take extra care in hiking, noticing turnoffs and return points. If in doubt, and if you lack a topographic map or map-reading skills, or have a poor sense of direction, retrace your hike back along the route you came in on if you sense that you are losing your way. Only well-seasoned and skilled hikers should attempt bushwhacking in an unknown area. Too often, one canyon or trail begins to look exactly like all the others.

The Living Desert and The Desert Museum

Located in Palm Desert and Palm Spr'ngs, respectively, these fine attractions offer informative exhibits and insights into the desert flora and fauna that you might see on one of your hikes. They are well worth visiting.

Area Maps and the National Forest Adventure Pass (NFAP)

Visitors using this book who want to supplement and expand their knowledge of the area will find Desert Map & Aerial Photo (73-612 Hwy. 111, Palm Desert, (760) 346-1101) the perfect resource for topographic maps and resource materials and for purchasing the NFAP. This pass permits you to park at trailheads in the Santa Rosa and San Jacinto mountains, whether on a daily basis or for a longer time frame with a yearly pass. The owners who operate Desert Map know the area as well as anyone, and are very helpful in directing you to any local trails that would fit your needs.

Index

Note: Citations followed by the letter "m" denote maps.

About the Author/Photographer

Philip Ferranti has hiked the western United States for over 20 years. He has spent much of that time exploring the trails in and near Palm Springs and the Coachella Valley. He founded the Coachella Valley Hiking Club in 1992, has written for *Backpacker* magazine, and is a frequent guest speaker at outdoor/hiking conventions. As president of Transformation Seminars since 1981, Philip specializes in seminars on stress management and hiking for health/wellness, and believes that hiking is one of the most effective, valuable stress management activities available. He has written six books, including *Hiking! The Ultimate Natural Prescription for Health & Wellness* (distributed by Westcliffe Publishers), and the regional best-selling books, *75 Great Hikes in and Near Palm Springs and the Coachella Valley* and *Colorado State Parks: A Complete Recreation Guide.* Philip summers in and hikes out of Boulder, Colorado.

Philip is available for slide shows, lectures, seminars, and guided hikes both in and near Palm Springs, and for longer packaged hiking vacations in Utah, Colorado, and the San Francisco Bay Area. Phone him at (760) 345-6234 or e-mail him at Pferran1@aol.com.

About the Cartographer

Hank Koenig is an avid hiker and self-avowed "techno-geek." He has hiked extensively in New England and the Northwest as well as in Southern California. He is a founding member and hike leader for the Coachella Valley Hiking Club. After a 30-year career as an electronics engineer for a major defense contractor, where he learned the theory and practice of GPS, Hank retired and turned his attention to his two favorite pursuits, hiking and electronics. During the summer he volunteers as a GPS Specialist for the Willamette National Forest at the McKenzie Ranger District in Central Oregon. He develops data for the construction of maps and trail inventories. Hank also trains staff from the national forests and the Bureau of Land Management in the Northwest in the practical use of GPS.